MINIMUM ESSENTIAL POLITENESS

MINIMUM ESSENTIAL POLITENESS

A Guide to the Japanese Honorific Language

by Agnes M. Niyekawa
University of Hawaii

KODANSHA INTERNATIONAL
Tokyo • New York • London

Distributed in the United States by Kodansha America, Inc., 114 Fifth Avenue, New York, N. Y. 10011, and in the United Kingdom and continental Europe by Kodansha Europe Ltd., 95 Aldwych, London WC2B 4JF. Published by Kodansha International Ltd., 17-14 Otowa 1-chome, Bunkyo-ku, Tokyo 112, and Kodansha America, Inc.

ISBN 4-7700-1624-7
First edition, 1991
93 10 9 8 7 6 5 4 3 2

Library of Congress Cataloging in Publication Data

Niyekawa, Agnes.
Minimum essential politeness: a guide to the Japanese
honorific language/by Agnes M. Niyekawa.—1st ed.
    p.   cm.
Includes bibliographical references.
ISBN 4-7700-1624-7
1. Japanese language—Honorific. I. Title.
PL629.H65N58 1991
495.6'82421—dc20   91-44628
                                                          CIP

Contents

VII. Review of Levels — 131

VIII. Current Trends — 146

Appendix: The *Keigo* System in Relation to the European V/T System — 151

PREFACE

Anyone who has learned Japanese as a foreign language would agree that *keigo*, the honorific language, is the most difficult part of Japanese. *Keigo* words like *irasshaimasu* or *orimasu* may be introduced one by one in the language text with the appropriate explanation each time, but one seldom gains an overview of the honorific system at the end of the language training. There has long been a need for a book that puts together bits and pieces of "polite expressions" to provide a picture of the whole.

This book was written to meet this need. It is directed to readers who have had two to three years of Japanese language training, and can already speak basic Japanese except for the feeling of insecurity when it comes to speaking politely.

I have met many who say that they have given up on *keigo* and hope to be excused for it because they are foreigners. They say it lightly because they are unaware of what a breach of etiquette the omission of *keigo* is. Not to use *keigo*, particularly to someone from whom one seeks guidance, assistance, or cooperation, is like showing up at a dinner party in beach wear. Not only does the partygoer insult the host, but he also makes a fool out of himself.

Keigo is by no means easy to learn. I remember with chagrin how I responded to the question "*Niyekawa-san mo irasshaimasu ka?*" with "*Hai, irasshaimasu*" in the days when I was struggling with Japanese after having been a monolingual German speaker for a number of years.

Even native speakers have difficulty with *keigo*. But the difficulty is no excuse to ignore *keigo*. Not to make any effort to master it is to disregard the most important aspect of interpersonal relationships in Japan. Such a person can easily be perceived as showing cultural arrogance, looking down on the Japanese.

The primary goal of this book is to enable the readers to avoid making blunders. The first and most important thing a foreigner needs to learn is how NOT to be impolite. Hence the title *Minimum Essential Politeness*. Of the many levels of politeness in Japanese, there is one level which can be used in almost any situation without insulting anyone. This minimum level of politeness is the focus of this book.

But speaking is only half of the conversation. An older woman, for example, may speak to you at a very high level of politeness. In order to understand what others are saying, you need to be exposed to a wide range of levels. For comprehension purposes, I have added sample sentences at levels of politeness higher than the minimum essential level. Once you have mastered the minimal essential level of politeness, you may choose to go back and learn to speak at the other levels also.

It is my belief that foreigners need not become completely Japanese. I feel that they are entitled to maintain their identity with their home country. While it is nice for the foreigner to behave like a Japanese and show a great deal of *enryo*, or reserve, in interacting with the Japanese, it is also just as nice or even nicer when the foreigner behaves naturally in his or her accustomed way—as long as no rude behavior is shown. In fact, some degree of spontaneity, which the Japanese have long lost in their over-ritualistic formal behavior, can be stimulating and instructive for the Japanese.

It is for this reason that this book emphasizes "how not to be rude" rather than "how to be polite." It is recommended that the book be read in the intended order, namely from Chapter 1 to the end. Each chapter builds on the material presented before it. In terms of learning how not to be rude, Chapter 5 on how to say "you" and "I" is actually more important than the preceding chapter on exalting and humbling words; the presentation is reversed because the sample sentences provided in Chapter 5 will not be fully comprehended, meaningwise as well as in terms of their significance in *keigo* usage, unless one is familiar with the content of Chapter 4.

I have arranged the book so that it can serve as a reference after a full reading. In case the reader will reexamine just one relevant section of the book, I have restated the most important rules in various different chapters at the risk of being redundant.

The Summary Guides at the ends of the rather lengthy and detailed Chapters 4, 5, and 6 are step-by-step guidelines for mastery. Once you have read through the chapter, use the Summary Guide to decide which sections to study first, and which to put off until you have mastered the essentials.

Chapter 7 is a Summary Guide for the whole book, and Chapter 8 describes the present state of *keigo* usage. To obtain an overview, the reader might glance through these last two chapters first.

In writing this book, I have consulted innumerable books and articles by Japanese scholars and authors. Even though I cite only a few, I would like to acknowledge my general indebtedness to them. In particular, I have benefited from Evangeline Dunbar's treatise on donatory verbs (Master's thesis at the University of Hawaii).

Many contributed to my efforts in writing this book. I wish to express my special gratitude to the Social Science Research Council in New York for the grant that enabled me to work on this book for half a year without outside interruption; to Dr. Howard Hibbett, Director of the Edwin O. Reischauer Institute of Japanese Studies at Harvard University, and his staff for providing the facilities and support during my grant period; and to my students at the University of Hawaii and the University of Vienna, whose questions directed my attention to specific aspects of the *keigo* system that needed some clarification. I am also indebted to Janice Omura, who edited an early version of the manuscript, and to Laura F. Jones, who did an admirable job in editing to produce the final version.

—Agnes M. Niyekawa
Honolulu, 1991

1. Why Use *Keigo*?

In any society, one varies one's speech according to the situation, setting, and whom one is speaking to. We do it so automatically that we are unconscious of the instantaneous decisions we are making—as long as we are in the context of our own society. Only when we find ourselves in an unusual situation, or in a foreign setting, do we ponder how to say something that would be socially acceptable, and only then do we become aware of the politeness factor.

In America, where equality and informality prevail more than in any other country, one can say, "Will you come to my party tomorrow?" to one's boss as well as to one's best friend. However, to assume that there are no gradations of politeness in American English is to make an overgeneralization.

Take, for instance, the request to have the salt shaker passed down to you at the table. At a picnic or at a fast-food establishment, when you are with a circle of close friends or family, it would be perfectly all right to say, "John, pass me the salt." In a slightly more formal setting, such as when guests are present, you might say, "Do you mind passing me the salt?" At a formal banquet, however, when the person sitting next to you is a distinguished person you just met, and at this moment is not looking in your direction, it may be more appropriate to make the request apologetic, such as, "I hate to bother you, but would you mind passing me the salt?" Using the last polite expression in the first setting may sound like a joke or sarcasm, while the second expression in the last setting may give the impression that the speaker is not refined and may be attending such a banquet for the first time. Obviously, one must select from a number of possibilities the expression that is most appropriate to the occasion. While only three expressions are given here, one can easily think of more than ten ways to make the same request even in American English.

The polite way of speaking in Japanese, then, is nothing unique. What makes it appear difficult is the fact that the polite way of saying things involves a number of grammatical categories, such as nouns, pronouns, and verbs, all of which have to be coordinated to the same level of politeness. Because of the complexity of the Japanese honorific language, one is tempted to give up studying it altogether, expecting to be excused as a foreigner when one makes a mistake.

Some mistakes will be easily overlooked. Others, however, will be taken as a personal affront. For example, inappropriate use of the word "you" can have serious consequences. I know of two such cases myself: in one, an American addressed her landlord with the common second person pronoun *anata*; in another, a European student used the same word to address the father of his host family, who was a doctor. In both cases, the addressee was so angered by this insult as to ask the foreigner to move out of the house immediately. Unfortunately for these foreigners, the word *anata* is introduced as the equivalent of "you" in most language texts, without reference to its narrow usage. Despite the 1952 recommendation by the Ministry of Education that *anata* be used as a formal "you," customary usage has lowered it to a level where it can be used only in addressing an intimate equal, someone distinctly younger or lower in status, or a complete stranger. Addressing someone who does not fall in these categories with the word *anata* thus becomes a serious insult.

An ordinary grammatical error made by the foreigner may simply seem cute to the Japanese, but an error in *keigo* tends to arouse an instantaneous emotional reaction. More frequently than the foreigner assumes, this sociolinguistic error is taken as an intentional personal insult. This is particularly so with regard to address terms. During the student revolts in the 1960s, students addressed high-ranking university administrators with terms used by gangsters to address their subordinates. It had an immediate and stabbing effect much like Anglo-Saxon curse words did in those days in America.

Considering the fact that even Westerners have been subjected to abrupt termination of friendship by Japanese due to unintended insults stemming from improper use of polite speech, the Westerner cannot just assume that he will be excused as a foreigner all the time. **An expression that lacks the proper respect can be as sharp as a sword in cutting someone down.** People react emotionally to the way others address them or speak to them, for the degree of politeness used in speech reflects the degree of respect accorded them by the speaker. The status-conscious Japanese, therefore, tends to be overly sensitive to how he is spoken to.

Let us take an example of a foreigner visiting a Japanese in his office with a particular request. Unable or unwilling to use *keigo,* the foreigner couches his request in language that sounds condescending. The Japanese thus insulted remains composed and does not show his anger outwardly, but says politely under some pretext that he is unable to assist. A person making any sort of request, whether it is for information, assistance, or cooperation, is expected to be even more humble and respectful than usual. When he speaks casually as though he is a close friend of the addressee, the Japanese might think, "Why should I be helpful to a person who does not think I deserve greater respect?" The foreigner, on the other hand, does not know why his request has been refused, and may conclude that it is the Japanese who is being uncooperative.

Certainly a non-Japanese is not expected to be completely facile in *keigo*, the honorific language. However, a minimum amount of knowledge as to how to speak and behave in relation to a Japanese who is not an intimate equal is expected if he has a certain degree of fluency in Japanese. The person who is fairly fluent, therefore, has to be all the more careful not to make a *faux pas*, which can have serious consequences.

In the early days of the Peace Corps, volunteers in Turkey had problems in getting cooperation from the villagers even though the volunteers could speak Turkish fluently. It turned out that while their predeparture orientation included a thorough training in the language, sufficient cultural training had not been given. Their improper behavior due to ignorance of the Turkish traditional culture was interpreted as intentional and malevolent by the villagers. **Most people assume that a person who speaks a foreign language fluently also knows the culture well. Hence when he does not follow some of the basic cultural rules, they naturally interpret it as an intentional violation of the customs. Showing deference or respect to a non-intimate conversational partner is one such basic rule in Japan.** To expect that one will be excused as a foreigner may therefore be not only optimistic but dangerous, since one's errors can be misinterpreted.

To avoid such misunderstandings while you are studying *keigo*, apologize ahead of time for possible rudeness stemming from your insufficient knowledge. Explain that you have not mastered it yet, but would appreciate being corrected when you do make a mistake (*Mada keigo (ga) yoku wakarimasen kara, shitsurei na iikata o suru ka mo shiremasen ga, oyurushi kudasai. Machigai o naoshite itadakemashitara, tasukarimasu ga . . .*). Such a humble attitude is likely to be well received, and you will probably receive all the cooperation you need.

As for the correction and help in *keigo*, you may not receive as much as you want, except from close friends, for it is difficult for anyone to say that respect to him should be expressed in such and such a way. Being polite often means not being frank. The Japanese prefer not to make negative comments verbally, but rather to communicate nonverbally. To learn to interpret the nonverbal message also requires time. One must therefore try to have one's eyes and ears wide open to perceive as much as possible of what is subtly communicated. The new perceptions required in learning to use the essentials of *keigo* are discussed in Chapter 2.

Among those who teach Japanese to non-native speakers of Japanese, there are those who try to have the learners speak exactly like native speakers. How close the foreigner's Japanese should approximate that of the native speaker, I feel, depends on the purpose for which he wants to put the language to use. As far as pronunciation is concerned, I personally feel that as long as the accent does not hinder communication, it is charming and serves as an identity marker of the speaker's country of origin. I do not feel that the foreigner's pronunciation has to approximate that of a native Japanese, although having the pitch accent correct is often important in order to be understood. However, when it comes to *keigo*, **any adult who is in Japan to carry out business or research must be able to use the minimum essential of** *keigo* **in order not to be rude to those from whom he seeks assistance and cooperation.** In the case of those who plan to live in Japan permanently, particularly those who have married into a Japanese family, it will become necessary to gradually increase facility in the use of *keigo* as it is absolutely essential for smooth interpersonal relations with a wide range of individuals in Japan.

$2.$ *Keigo* in Japanese Society

The first step in learning to speak Japanese appropriately is to develop a new perception of the Japanese social structure as it relates to the Japanese language. Language texts often point out that a particular form is to be used in speaking to a person of higher status without explaining what higher status is. Naturally, the learner thinks in terms of his own society and does not use the form when speaking to someone he considers his equal, though in Japan the same person is actually of higher status. Many errors in *keigo* stem from this type of misunderstanding.

One must develop a new way of looking at things. In the new system of perception one must learn: 1) to see the individual in terms of whether or not he is of higher status than oneself; 2) to recognize whether or not he is to be treated as an in-group or out-group member; 3) to see actions carried out on behalf of someone as a "gift" and speak in terms of giving and receiving an action; and 4) to observe the slightest changes in expression for cues in nonverbal communication.

Status and Hierarchy

The Japanese are an extremely status-conscious people. **Despite the postwar democratization, rank hierarchy is strictly observed, in some cases more strictly than in prewar days.** As

Chie Nakane so aptly states in her book *Japanese Society*, there are no two people who can be considered completely equal in Japan. Even the most minute difference results in status difference within a group, and when someone who considers himself higher in status is not treated accordingly, a dire consequence can be the result.

The Japanese are used to seeing people in terms of status. From kindergarten, if not earlier at home, they are inculcated to show respect to those older than they are. Children bow and speak politely not only to all adults, but also to upperclassmen in school. To foreigners, particularly those from the United States where the category of "equals" is very broad, this way of classifying individuals into higher, equal, and lower status may go against the grain. However, if one wants to learn to speak Japanese appropriately without insulting the addressee, one must learn to perceive others according to the Japanese way of ranking, and be especially careful when interacting with those who should be accorded the higher status.

The observance of status difference is reflected not only in speech but also in other behavior. As Nakane says, "in everyday affairs a man who has no awareness of relative rank is not able to speak or even sit and eat." Going through the door to enter a room or elevator is by rank. When two people of approximately equal status behave politely, each may attempt to let the other enter the elevator or the car first. In such cases, because it is more polite not to give in easily, each may insist on deferring to the other, with no action taking place for a minute or so, a scene often observed in Japan. Seating arrangement is also by rank, whereby the guest of honor or the highest-ranking person is seated farthest away from the doorway, or with his back to the *tokonoma* (the alcove with a scroll hanging), if it is a Japanese room. One does not touch one's food until the highest-ranking person has started to eat. Similarly, in conferences, one does not speak up before others higher in status have spoken, unless it is made clear at the beginning or through some policy that people should speak up freely.

At home, taking a bath is also by rank order. The bathwater is not changed throughout the evening, and everyone soaks in the same water after having thoroughly cleansed himself outside the tub. Nevertheless, the bathwater becomes less clear with subsequent baths, and it is only natural then that the highest-status person should be the first to take his bath and soak in clear water. In the days when the Japanese family consisted of three generations with many children, the order was generally by age within each sex group, women's turns coming only after the last man had finished, with smaller children bathing with their grandmother or mother. When there is a houseguest, the houseguest is given the highest status, and precedes all the others. Because the Japanese like the bath to be hot, bath-taking has to be done in rapid succession. This means that when the guest is told the bath is ready, he should take his bath immediately, for all the others are waiting in line.

DETERMINANTS OF STATUS

As in most other societies, **rank and position, social status, age, and sex** are factors to be taken into consideration in determining the hierarchy. Of these, age can be hardest to guess. Many Westerners have difficulty accurately judging the age of Japanese, perceiving the Japanese to be much younger than they actually are. The major reason is that one uses the clues one has learned in one's native culture to estimate the age of people in other cultures, where these clues do not necessarily apply. These clues have not been taught, but learned unconsciously through exposure and experience. For this reason, they are hard to enumerate verbally. Take for instance wrinkles in the face. Most middle-aged Japanese do not have the deep lines on the forehead that begin to show among Americans in their twenties when they frown.

Additionally, there are other socio-cultural factors that contribute to the underestimation of a Japanese individual's age by the Westerner. (Conversely, Westerners, particularly the younger ones, are sometimes taken for being older than they actually are by the Japanese.)

One factor is that the Japanese culture emphasizes dependence over independence, group over the individual self, resulting in a slow development of social poise associated with self-confidence.

Since the average Japanese socializes mainly within intimate circles of friends from work, school, or community, without trying to make new friends, he is shy and uncomfortable in interaction with strangers, giving the impression to Westerners that he is socially immature, and thus younger than his age.

It is not uncommon for a Westerner to be off by more than ten years in estimating how old a Japanese person is. Since age is associated with rank and status, an underestimation of age by ten years can mean treating a higher-status person as having lower status—very rude behavior indeed. Of course, as one gets to know the person and his past better, one can more accurately estimate his age. It is not considered polite to ask directly how old the addressee is. The Japanese often get around to it by bringing up the topic of *juunishi* (the cycle of 12 animals in Chinese zodiac). One might say that he himself was born in the year of horse or whatever, and then ask, *X-san* (or *sensei*) *wa nanidoshi umare de irasshaimasu ka?* (Which animal year were you born in?)

Work Settings. Length of service, namely **seniority**, tends to weigh more heavily than age. Thus, other things being equal, a person who started to work at the same place one year or even just a few months earlier has the higher status, and must be treated as a *sempai* (literally "more experienced person"), or a *meue* ("senior"), by the less experienced *koohai*, or *meshita* ("junior"). Women clerks (*jimuin* or "O.L." for "office ladies") often are placed in a separate lower category in this rank ordering.

When a group of several fresh university graduates are hired, and they enter the company at the same time, they are *doohai* ("colleagues of the same age" or "cohorts"), and are basically equal. However, gradually a subtle hierarchy is likely to develop at least between pairs of individuals in the group, if not among the whole group. The individual who is a year older is of higher status. It often does not matter if his being older is due to the fact that he failed the entrance examination to the university and entered it a year later on his second try. In addition, an individual from a high-ranked university is often accorded higher status as well. This type of subtle ranking among *doohai*, however, is not likely to be reflected in speech. They will speak to one another at the same level of politeness. Still, the minute difference in status will enable the person slightly higher in status, if he so chooses, to dominate the lower-status person in minor matters, because the latter will defer to him.

One can expect factors to cross: based on one factor, A is of higher status, but based on another factor, B is higher. When determining factors are at variance in the workplace, rank and position weigh more heavily than other factors. If the section chief is younger or is a woman, those working under him or her still have to show due respect. The young boss may speak slightly more politely to an older employee than he would to other younger employees. Not long ago a rather surprising murder case surfaced in the news. An employee had killed his slightly younger boss because he could no longer take being spoken down to. There are ways to reduce friction and embarrassment in situations like this, such as each being polite to the other.

University Setting. Universities are highly structured organizations where hierarchy plays as important a role as at the workplace. Rank and seniority are the major determinants of the hierarchy. Students rank lower than the teachers, as in any other country. In Japan, however, hierarchy based on seniority is observed among students, especially within smaller groups on campus, such as in clubs. As a consequence, students often speak more politely to their upperclassmen than to their teachers. At many schools today, students speak to their teachers informally as if they are friends. At the university level, where students are expected to behave more like adults and show respect to their professors, speaking informally to the professor is not as widespread as at elementary and secondary school levels. Thus, whether or not one may speak informally to the professor depends on the university. The general rule, however, is to observe the hierarchy and to show respect in speech and behavior to all professors.

Loosely Structured or Non-Structured Settings. While status difference is strictly observed in settings like school and the workplace where everybody's status position is clear, in less structured settings and organizations there is less of a compulsion to rank order individual members. The officers and leaders of a club or loosely formed organization are generally treated with respect by the other members, but this does not necessarily mean that they lord over the others and speak down to them. In PTAs, neighborhood groups, social clubs, and so forth, people speak cordially to one another at the formal level. However, because there are fine gradations within the formal level in Japanese, it is possible to show greater or less respect or even subtle condescension while speaking politely. If the addressee is known to have a high social status, one may speak to him slightly more politely than to another who does not.

First Meetings. At a first meeting between individuals who do not know each other's age, occupation, or social status, and when business cards are not exchanged, people interact as non-intimate (out-group) equals by exchanging polite speech. Rank order is established only when there is an obvious difference, such as sex, age difference of more than ten years, great difference in implied social status or socio-economic background based on clothes and appearance, as well as speech as an index of educational and regional background.

When there are obvious differences, the higher-status person may or may not speak down to the lower-status person. Which option the higher-status person takes depends a great deal on the personality of the speaker. Men generally tend to speak downwards. Women usually speak at a higher level of politeness than men, and do not speak downwards except to children and household help, while men tend to speak down to women and children as well as anyone who appears to be lower in status. I have had the experience on a train in Japan where the "stranger" next to me, with whom I had been talking for half an hour, suddenly changed his manner and speech, and apologized for his rudeness upon discovering that I was a university professor in America. Such a sudden change would not have been necessary had he not been slightly speaking down to me because I was a woman.

Favors. A determinant of a temporary nature is favors. Between two individuals more or less equal in status, the recipient of a big favor is lower in status until a similar favor is returned. If a higher-status person, such as a former teacher or boss, is the recipient of a big favor, let us say a loan of a considerable sum of money, he will assume a humble posture in relation to the lower-status person who did him the favor of lending him the money.

Race. The hierarchically oriented Japanese like to rank order everything from people, universities, and brand-name products to races. Sometimes ethnicity seems to weigh more heavily than sex and age in ranking individuals. Caucasians rank at the top, above the Japanese themselves, when it comes to service at hotels and restaurants, while in legal matters involving rights, they may be discriminated against as aliens. The Japanese consider themselves to be at the top among people of color—Asians and Africans. Hence when nothing else is known about the individual, the Caucasian is generally given preferential treatment with some degree of respect, while the non-Caucasian foreigner, whether a foreigner of Japanese ancestry—Japanese American, Japanese Canadian, Japanese Brazilian, and so forth—or of any other Asian extraction, is often treated with some condescension.

Because Japan is such a homogeneous country, where language, culture, and race coincide, many Japanese have a mystical belief in "blood," and feel that anybody who has Japanese blood flowing in his body should think, speak, and behave the Japanese way. Anyone who is racially Japanese but does not meet this expectation because of a different cultural background is often looked upon as if he is somehow retarded and is thus discriminated against in an anonymous situation. Fortunately this situation appears to be gradually improving with the increased presence of Japanese Americans in different geographical areas in Japan.

Long-Term Relationships. The Westerner often assumes that with long association and the development of closer relationship, the strict hierarchy breaks down. That is not the case in Japan. Unless the two individuals are nearly equal in age and status from the start, **duration of friendship usually does not change a senior-junior relationship to an "equal" one** in which they can mutually speak informally. No matter how frequently they see each other, the degree of politeness to be used in speech does not change, even though the content of conversation may include more jokes. The junior person is not permitted to speak informally to the senior person throughout his lifetime once the relationship is established. Thus someone who has become a well-known writer or even the prime minister will still speak with respect to his grade school teacher at a class reunion, although the teacher's manner of speech may show respect for him and be polite.

SUMMARY

The strong traditional emphasis on rank seems to account for the continued observance of these rules of etiquette in speech and in behavior. Because the younger are lower in status, they have no choice but to observe the established norm of behavior when they join a group where the elder and the more experienced have the power. Considering the fact that these rules are strictly observed among high school and university students, particularly in sports clubs, there seems to be little hope that the observation of hierarchy will fade away in the near future.

The important thing to remember is to observe the hierarchy in interacting with individuals from school or work. With *non-intimate* individuals outside these groups, hierarchy does not play as conspicuous a role, because one generally relates to the out-group person with politeness unless he or she is distinctly lower in status.

Group

The Japanese generally derive their identity from the group they belong to. When asked what they do, the Japanese frequently respond by saying they work for such and such a company, rather than by giving their occupation. Men wear the company badge on their lapels every day. Women clerical workers in many companies wear a uniform, a type of smock, at work. Strong identification with the company and uniformity of behavior are some of the most important values an employee must uphold.

The **exchange of business cards** when two individuals first meet has been frequently used as an example of the need among the Japanese to establish a rank order. Actually, however, the business card usually provides only the person's name, the organization and division he works in, and the organization's address and telephone number. It seldom provides the exact position he holds, unless he is a higher-ranking official of the organization. Frequently, then, two individuals can exchange business cards and still be none the wiser as to rank, except that the person who is affiliated with the better-known company has the higher status. One derives one's status partly from group affiliation.

More importantly than establishing rank, the business card functions to help commit to memory the name of the new acquaintance. The Japanese need to see the name in writing because of the many homophones in the language. The same name *Takeshita*, for instance, can be written using a number of different *kanji*. On the other hand, the same two-character name may have different readings.

More often than not, name cards are not exchanged to establish rank order. This is because regardless of rank, when two individuals who do not belong to the same company speak to each other, particularly in business negotiations, each must speak politely and with respect to the other. Each treats the other as if the other were higher in rank. This mutually deferential treatment is the basic rule in interaction with an out-group person, a point we will come back to again and again in this book.

Group Orientation. Group identity, or the awareness of the group one belongs to, is inculcated in the Japanese from early childhood. The child is constantly reminded that behaving inappropriately will bring shame to his family, the group he belongs to. Thus the idea that he is not responsible only to himself, but to his group is introduced to him well before he enters school. The child carries the burden of representing his family through his last name, and his school through his school uniform or badge. Winning in competitive sports activities on the school athletic day (*undookai*), or recognition of excellence in any field, brings honor to the class or the school the individual is a member of. One competes to bring honor to one's group rather than for oneself. If an individual takes the honor personally and does not share it with the group, or does not credit the group for having given him the moral support that enabled him to win the competition, he is considered one who destroys the harmony (*wa*) of the group and thus an undesirable member. As an old saying goes, the fence post that sticks out gets pounded in (*Deru kui wa utareru*).

GROUP ORIENTATION IN LANGUAGE

This group orientedness is strongly reflected in Japanese speech, particularly in polite speech. Polite speech is considered a lubricant, often described as a way to reduce friction among the multitude of people populating this crowded island country. In interacting with someone who does not belong to one's group, namely a *yoso* (out-group) person, one treats him as if he is of higher status. Thus in a non-intimate setting, it is best to be polite and respectful to the people one is interacting with. **Humble oneself and exalt the addressee is the basic rule, but "self" includes members of the speaker's group, while the "addressee" includes members of the addressee's group.** A major portion of the rules of honorific speech has to do with this *uchi* ("in-group" or "my group") and *yoso* ("out-group" or "your group") distinction.

In general, an out-group member is treated in the same way as a person of higher status, except a complete stranger, *aka no tanin*, who is treated with indifference. In other words, each behaves deferentially and addresses the other with respect (Diagram 1a). This is quite different from an interaction situation where one who actually has the higher status speaks down to the lower status person, while the lower status person speaks up to him (Diagram 1b).

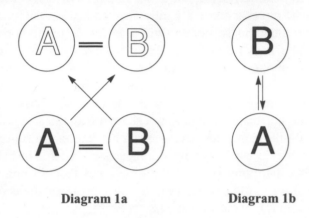

Diagram 1a   Diagram 1b

Family. A basic example of this in-group/out-group distinction is found in **kinship terminology**. A father is addressed, for instance, in a number of ways, *o-too-san*, *o-too-chan*, *too-chan*, etc., varying greatly according to families. The point to be made here is that one always *addresses* family members who are one's senior with an honorific suffix (*-san*, *-chan*). But when one *refers* to one's father in speaking to someone outside the family, namely an out-group person, one refers to him plainly as *chichi*, a humbling term in reference to one's own father. On the other hand, in referring to someone else's father, especially that of the addressee, one must exalt him by attaching the honorific prefix *o-* and suffix *-sama* or *-san*, and say *o-too-sama* or *o-too-san*. This distinction makes it superfluous to say "*watashi no*" (my) *chichi*, since *chichi* in speech can mean only "my" (the speaker's) father. In stricter families, children learn to make this distinction while still in elementary school. Those who continue into their adulthood to refer to their own family members using honorifics when speaking to an out-group person are considered poorly educated or as having a lower socioeconomic background.

In addition to these kinship terms, there is a host of other nouns and verbs that have "humbling" or "exalting" meanings, as well as grammatical devices which change neutral words to exalting or humbling equivalents. In order to show respect to the addressee, the exalting terms must be applied to the addressee and members of the addressee's group, and the humbling terms to the speaker and members of his group. Chapter 4 will address these terms in more detail.

Place of Work as Group. The family concept extends to one's place of work. A trend that has become increasingly stronger in postwar years is to apply the same in-group/out-group or "our" vs. "your" distinction to the speech of company employees. Within the company, how politely one speaks and how much respect one shows to the addressee are strictly determined by the hierarchy discussed previously. However, when speaking to someone outside the company, such as in the case of responding to a telephone call from outside, or receiving a visitor, the hierarchy within the company is completely ignored, and the in-group/out-group distinction comes into play. The out-group person is treated with respect, and in-group members, even one's own boss or the president of the company, is treated as one would treat oneself, namely in a humbling fashion. This means referring to one's boss without using honorifics, and speaking of him like one's family member when talking to the outsider.

Exaltation of "you and members of your group," and humbling of "myself and members of my group" are required mainly when one represents one's group in business, conferences, and negotiations. This is particularly prominent in the speech of sales and service personnel when speaking to customers and clients. However, in non-commercial settings like educational and research institutions and hospitals, reference to in-group members of rank is often not done with humble expressions. A nurse referring to the doctor will use exalting terms for him in speaking to a patient or visitor. Thus there are some exceptions to the rule of treating an in-group member with humble expressions while exalting the out-group member.

The Foreigner as Out-Group Member. A visitor or a guest is always treated cordially as an out-group member. Thus, aside from the supposed racial hierarchies, the polite speech by which the non-Japanese individual, particularly a Caucasian, is addressed may be more that to an out-group member rather than that used when addressing a person actually higher in status. The Westerner who has had it pounded into his head that Japanese polite speech and behavior are based on status difference, and who is not familiar with the etiquette involved in interactions with an out-group member, often misinterprets the respect he is accorded. He considers himself to be of higher status and may unconsciously come to take a patronizing attitude toward the Japanese.

SUMMARY

The important thing to remember here is that the individual does not stand alone, but is always a member of some group. Members of the individual's family are always treated in the same way as he treats himself, and when he represents his company, he must refer to members of his company as he would his family, using humble expressions, while on the other hand exalting members of the addressee's group. In other words, **in a cross-group interaction situation, the hierarchy within the in-group is ignored in speech, and group membership supersedes hierarchy as a determinant in the use of** *keigo*.

Gifts or Favors

The third area in which a new perception and interpretation are essential for the foreigner has to do with giving and receiving. The Japanese are caught up in an interpersonal network of obligations called *giri*. They owe *giri* (become obligated) to those who have done them favors, and they try to repay their obligations in kind. Gift giving is a way they express their gratitude for the favors received. It is a significant part of the rituals involved in the everyday lives of the Japanese. The Japanese give gifts twice annually to people to whom they are permanently obligated, such as their boss, their close *sempai*s, their doctors and dentists, their own or their children's teachers, their go-between in marriage, etc. Not only are the Japanese constantly involved in gift giving, but they also express actions carried out for the sake of others, or actions carried out on their behalf by others, in terms of giving or receiving.

Dependence on Others. While younger people are becoming increasingly independent, the Japanese in general show a strong tendency toward dependence on others. They tend to attribute their successes as well as failures, at least in part, to others or to fate, as if they themselves could not carry out anything on their own. Knowing the right people, namely *kone* (from the word "connection"), who can wield influence in times of need, therefore, is considered very important. This dependence on the favor of others, and appreciation when such favors are done, find expression in the donatory verb. In Japanese, one does not say "He wrote a letter of recommendation for me," but "He did me the favor of writing a letter of recommendation." Even small favors, such as your brother buying the evening paper on his way home for you, is expressed as "giving me the action of buying the paper." To use such an expression with the donatory verb requires becoming sensitive to actions done on behalf of others. In other words, it requires a new perspective.

Donatory Verbs. The verbs used to express the act of giving or receiving objects, as in "The teacher gave me a book," are called donatory verbs. A donatory verb can be combined with another verb to form a compound verb that describes favors done for others or favors received. The favor is thus expressed as a "gift" of action.

To give a few examples, a simple statement like "Will you drop these letters in the mailbox on your way?" requires the use of a donatory verb even in speaking to an intimate. In Japanese it comes out "Won't you *give me* the favor of dropping these letters in the mail box on your way?" (*Yuubinbako ni kono tegami (o) tookan shite itte kurenai?* or *Posuto ni kono tegami (o) tookan shite itte ku-*

dasaranai?) Similarly the statement "The book you loaned me is very interesting" has to be restated in Japanese to "The book which you gave me (or which I received) the favor of loaning is very interesting." (*Kashite kureta/moratta hon (wa) totemo omoshiroi* or *Okashi kudasatta/itadaita go-hon (wa) totemo omoshirou gozaimasu,* etc.) There are seven or eight commonly used donatory verbs; one simply chooses the one appropriate to the level of speech one is using, which is determined by the status relationship between the speaker and the addressee or the group membership of each.

Group membership, which was discussed earlier, enters into the picture here again when the statement is something like "Your sister read fairy tales to my son." "Your sister" is treated the same way as "you," and "my son" as "I myself." The choice of donatory verb in this case, therefore, is based on the relationship between "you" and "I," namely the speaker and the addressee, and not on the relationship between giver and receiver of the act of reading.

The rules governing the choice of donatory verbs will be discussed in Chapter 6. Suffice it to state here that **any action carried out for the sake of someone else is interpreted as "a gift of action" and generally requires the use of a donatory verb.** The action may not even be an intentional favor—if it can be perceived as having a favorable consequence to the speaker, it is expressed with a donatory verb. Even the final silence of an incessant chatterer might be described as "*Yatto damatte kureta*" ("He/she finally did me the favor of silencing" meaning "Thank goodness, he/she finally shut up"). Reorienting one's perspective to interpret actions in terms of giving and receiving is the first step toward the appropriate use of the donatory verb.

Nonverbal and Vague Communication

Nonverbal communication plays an extremely important role in Japanese society. It is said that the real feeling of the speaker is expressed more frequently nonverbally. For instance, a person may verbally agree when nonverbal cues suggest otherwise. In such a case, it is the nonverbal message that carries the true meaning.

Such cues, however, are not easy to perceive for people who have not grown up in Japan. The foreigner should watch for the slightest change in facial expression or flow of speech, and for restless body movements in the partner. What such behavior means would depend on the situation. It may be a response to the content of speech or the manner in which the words were said. It takes a long time of careful observation to learn the cues. Japanese children who were raised abroad, including myself, are often criticized for being slow in catching these nonverbal cues, and receive complaints from their close friends that they do not get the message unless everything is stated overtly and clearly.

The use of euphemism and circumlocution in polite speech is a sociolinguistic universal. In Japan, however, this sort of vagueness also has an aesthetic value. Hence indirect speech has a double value in Japan. A frequent device used to give that sense of vagueness is to leave the sentence incomplete.

The style of communication even among family members and close friends is often indirect and vague. It is taken for granted that people close to you and who are in daily contact with you know what your habits and preferences are, and need not be given elaborate explanations. A person who is too exact, direct, and detailed is considered unsophisticated. Such direct speech can be taken as an insult to the intelligence of the addressee.

In cross-cultural communication, however, there is the danger that a vague statement might be interpreted differently from the intended message of the speaker due to the fact that people of different cultures operate under different assumptions. For this reason, I personally feel that **it is important for the non-native speaker to learn to read nonverbal cues, but not necessarily to use vague and indirect communication,** at least not in the early stages of his stay in Japan. There is too much risk for possible misunderstanding. I also feel that the foreigner is entitled to maintain his identity and speak directly and frankly in the manner he is used to in his native tongue. In fact, it is often found to be charming and refreshing when foreigners do so with such innocence.

As can be seen, my position is not to make a Japanese out of a non-Japanese. As mentioned in the Preface, the emphasis of this book is on minimum level of politeness for active production, and a wide range of speech levels for passive comprehension.

3. The *Keigo* System

Now that we have seen which circumstances require the use of honorifics in reference to which individuals, we are ready to examine how the *keigo* system actually works. Respect is not merely expressed by choosing a polite form over a nonpolite one; there are many gradations in *keigo* speech, and differing dimensions as well. This chapter will begin by defining the basic terms used in this text. Then we will closely examine several different gradations of the same sentence for an overview of the various components of *keigo* and the four main levels of speech. The chapter will conclude with some additional notes about Japanese culture that affect speech at specific levels.

Terminology

Keigo. The term *keigo* has two meanings in Japanese: in the broader sense it refers to the whole system of honorific language, and in the narrower sense it refers to individual words and morphemes (part of a word that carries meaning, such as prefix, suffix, etc.) used to express politeness. In this book, *keigo* will refer to the system as a whole, while the term "honorifics" or "*keigo* words" will be used to refer to the narrower meaning. Today the *keigo* system is frequently referred to by the term *taiguu hyoogen*, which means "the linguistic treatment of self and others in conversation."

Japanese grammarians have generally classified the system into three large categories of *keigo* words: (1) *sonkei-go* or "exalting words"; (2) *kenjoo-go* or "humbling words"; and (3) *teinei-go* or "polite words." The first two categories are fairly clear-cut with little ambiguity, but the third category is essentially a wastebasket category—any word or part of a word with some meaning of politeness, which are neither (1) nor (2), fall into this category, including *desu/-masu*, which in this text is treated separately as "style." There obviously is room for further classification, and many grammarians have done so.

But classification into groups of words does not give a clear picture of how the *keigo* system works as a whole. I will therefore deviate considerably from the traditional treatment of *keigo* in hopes of making the system easier for non-Japanese to understand.

Style. First is the notion of style. Every Japanese sentence bears either the *da* style or the *desu/-masu* style. The distinction between the two styles is fundamental to the *keigo* system. Sentences with the formal *desu/-masu* ending, or with a derivative ending such as *deshita*, *-masen*, or *-mashoo*, are *desu/-masu*-style sentences; those without the ending are informal *da*-style sentences. We will refer to the *desu/-masu* style as P, for polite, and the *da* style as N, for nonpolite.

These two styles have variously been called formal vs. informal, formal vs. plain, polite vs. plain, etc. by various scholars in the West. In this book, "formality," "respect," "refinement," and "politeness," will be distinguished as follows. They are presented only for the purpose of more accurate description.

Formality. Formality will refer to the style, thus the P/N distinction: the *da* style being "informal" and the *desu/-masu* style being "formal." The term "formal," however, will occasionally be used in reference to words. For instance, *honjitsu* is the formal word for *kyoo*, meaning today. Formal speech in Japanese uses many Chinese compounds with *on* (Chinese sound) readings. *Honjitsu* is one of them. Although such Chinese compounds tend to appear in more polite speech, one cannot say that *honjitsu* is more polite, or more respectful. It is used more frequently in writing, which usually is more formal than speech. Generally, the more politely one speaks, the more formal the speech becomes. Thus there is a correlation between formality and politeness, but this does not make "formality" synonymous with "politeness."

Respect. Part of being polite is showing respect to the other person. In Japanese speech, this is accomplished by creating a distance between the speaker and the addressee. The formal *desu/-masu* style accomplishes this only minimally. By employing lexical and grammatical devices to elevate the addressee and lower the speaker, one can create an even greater distance, and make the speech that much more respectful. "Respect," as used here, will refer to "exalting" the addressee, and "humbling" the speaker, and "respect words" will refer to all those words and morphemes which accomplish one of these functions. The fact that the "exalting" and "humbling" words comprise two of the three *keigo* categories in the traditional Japanese classification of *keigo* indicates the major role these words play in the honorific language system.

Refinement. There are words, supposedly neutral, that are used only by men in informal speech, such as *sushi*, *bentoo* (box lunch), *hashi* (chopsticks), etc. These words are considered to be too crude to be used in polite speech, and at any time by women, who speak more politely than men. Thus the prefix *o-* is attached to make them sound less crude, like *o-sushi*, *o-hashi*. There are set prefixes and suffixes that make neutral words more refined when attached to them. There are also substitutes for common neutral words, such as *dochira* for *doko* ("where") and *dore* ("which"), or *kochira* for *kore* ("this"). These words, although associated with polite speech, are neither "formal" nor related to "respect." They will be referred to as words of "refinement."

Politeness. In this text, the term "politeness" will be used mainly in reference to *degree* of politeness at the sentence level. As mentioned before, there are many gradations within the *desu/-masu* style. A sentence may be more "polite" than another because it uses more *keigo* words. The degree of "politeness" is determined by the combination of style (P or N) and the use (or non-use) of words of respect, formality (such as Chinese compounds), and refinement.

It is not essential to be able to make these distinctions in order to learn to speak politely. There are, however, occasions, such as in delivering a speech to an audience, when "formality" and "respect" are called for, but not necessarily "refinement."

The Two Styles

HIERARCHY AND GROUP

Now, let's examine style through what we know about the Japanese culture. The Japanese choose between the informal *da* style and the formal *desu/-masu* style based on the relationship between the speaker and the addressee. Hierarchy and group affiliation, as discussed in the previous chapter, are the two main dimensions involved in the use of the P/N system. The important point to keep in mind is that in hierarchical situations, P/N is used non-reciprocally, while in group situations, either N or P is used reciprocally.

The **hierarchy** dimension dictates that the person of higher status is entitled to use the *da* style to the person of lower status, while the latter must use the *desu/-masu* style in speaking to the former. Remember that in any hierarchically structured organization a one-year difference in age, length of service, or class standing in school results in a junior-senior status difference. Thus,

Senior: *Ano repooto yonda ka?* (Did you read that report?)
Junior: *Hai, yomimashita.* (Yes, I read it.)

In this context, the nonpolite *da* style, or N, can be said to be the style of condescension, and the polite *desu/-masu* style, or P, the style of reverence (see Appendix).

The **group** dimension affects style by defining a narrow group of intimates around the speaker. The *da* style is used reciprocally among family members and classmates and thus is the style of intimacy, while the *desu/-masu* style used mutually among non-intimates (out-group members) is the style of formality. The *da* style is the language with which children grow up. Not only do parents, grandparents, and elder siblings speak to the child in the *da* style, but the child too speaks to elder members of the family in the *da* style in most families today. Obviously, within the family, intimacy wins out over hierarchy in the style choice, resulting in a mutual *da* style. The child continues to use the *da* style in speaking to his classmates from kindergarten to college, but not to upperclassmen. Anyone of higher status outside the family must be spoken to in the *desu/-masu* style. The teacher seems to be an exception. In his effort to instill democratic behavior in the students, and in playing the role of a friendly mentor, today's teacher seems to accept being spoken to by his students in the *da* style, something that was not permitted and was considered to be the teacher's responsibility to correct in prewar days.

Except in the family, in any in-group situation—school group or workplace—hierarchy is the determinant of level of speech. However, a person who is not a member of any of the speaker's groups, hierarchical or intimate, is always spoken to in P, the formal *desu/-masu* style. This holds true for the other person too, hence they will exchange mutual P. The importance of making a distinction between in-group and out-group members in speech will become clearer as we go deeper into the honorific language system of Japanese.

The N Style. The nonpolite *da* style is used only within the family and among intimate equals as the style for "intimacy," or in speaking to someone *clearly* younger or lower in status within a hierarchical group as the style of "condescension." In all other situations, P, the *desu/-masu* style, is used. It is because of the rather limited use of the *da* style that the adult foreigner learning Japanese is normally taught to speak the formal *desu/-masu* style. Unless the foreigner enters a school in Japan, where the *da* style is in use among fellow classmates, or enters an organization at the executive level, he will have few opportunities to use the *da* style until he develops close friendships.

With acquaintances made in the world of *shakaijin* (responsible adults), the use of N-level speech comes only after the relationship develops into close friendship when the two parties involved happen to have equal status. Drinking parties often lead to N-level speech, since in Japan one is excused of all rude behavior when one is drunk, but the partygoers generally revert back to P-level speech when sober. For this reason, it is extremely important to distinguish the N-level speech based on hierarchy from that on intimacy. N-level speech coming from a close friend is based on intimacy, and thus is reciprocal. You would respond in N also. If, however, the N comes from someone who is higher in status, it is based on hierarchy, and therefore is not reciprocal. You must respond in P. As pointed out earlier, your *meue* can say *anata* or *kimi* to you, but as *meshita* you cannot use *anata* to him.

The P Style: Basic Politeness. The *desu/-masu* style, the P of "reverence" and "formality," connotes politeness to some extent by creating a distance between the speaker and addressee through formality. One would use the *desu/-masu* style in speaking to a stranger, a non-intimate equal, or an out-group member, as well as to someone older or higher in status than oneself. Not using the *desu/-masu* style in these situations will be interpreted as being fresh, rude, and arrogant. Some Americans acquire fluency in Japanese while they are high school exchange students in Japan and manage fine as high school students with just the *da* style. If they do not receive further training in the Japanese language on their return to America, they remain arrested at the *da* style of speech. Unaware of the sociolinguistic rules on politeness, and fully confident of their fluency, they approach Japanese professors on American campuses and speak to them in N. Such speech appears to be childish for a college student, and extremely rude considering the fact that they are speaking to a professor.

To show respect, however, and to be really polite to someone higher in status, one must do more than just use the *desu*/-*masu* style. One must use other honorific words in combination with the *desu*/-*masu* ending. In other words, the *desu*/-*masu* ending by itself proves only that the speaker is sufficiently polite not to treat the addressee as someone lower in status.

Gradations of Politeness. The fine gradations, mainly within P, in Japanese are made possible by employing various devices. Generally the more polite the level of speech, the more devices used. To show respect to the addressee, one exalts the addressee while at the same time humbling oneself. One also uses more "formal" and "refined" words as the degree of politeness increases.

It is also possible to be informal in N and at the same time show respect, such as *Anata mo irassharu?* ("Will you come too?") where *irassharu* is an exalting word showing respect, but in the *da* style. On the other hand, one can be formal, using the *desu*/-*masu* style, without using any other honorifics and thus show minimal respect to the addressee, as in *Mata kita n(o) desu ka?* ("You came again?"). These two examples, I hope, explain why we had to distinguish between the concepts of "politeness" and "formality," as well as between "formality" and "respect."

Levels of Politeness

Traditionally, three levels of politeness have been identified based on sentence style: the "plain" or nonpolite *da* level, the polite *desu*/-*masu* level, and the ultra-polite *gozaimasu* level. In this book, we will refer to these three levels as follows: "N" for the *da* level, "P-0" and "P-1" for the *desu*/-*masu* level, and "P-2" for the *gozaimasu* level. The *desu*/-*masu* level is divided into two levels to distinguish the neutral *desu*/-*masu* style P-0 that is taught in most language texts from the *desu*/-*masu* style P-1 that expresses respect to the addressee. P-0, P-1, and P-2 together will be referred to as "P." As mentioned earlier, all P sentences end in a derived form of *desu*/-*masu*, such as *desu, deshita, deshoo* or -*masu*, -*mashita*,

-masen, *mashoo*, **including** *gozaimasu*, and thus are easily distinguishable from N-level sentences with a plain verb ending.

The distinction between P-0 and P-1 is also not difficult. While sentences at both these levels end in *desu*/*-masu* style, a P-1 sentence contains some respect or polite expression while a P-0 sentence does not. Such a clear-cut distinction does not exist between P-1- and P-2-level sentences when the P-2 sentence does not end in *gozaimasu*. *Gozaimasu* is the formal equivalent of *arimasu*, and *de gozaimasu* is equivalent to *desu*. Thus not all sentences at the P-2 or *gozaimasu* level end in *gozaimasu*. In the absence of *gozaimasu*, the distinction between P-1 and P-2 levels can be made only in terms of degree of politeness expressed in the sentence. P-2 sentences generally employ a greater variety of devices to express politeness than P-1 sentences. The fact that there are so many gradations within P makes it all the more difficult to draw a line between P-1 and P-2 sentences, as the following list of gradational sentences indicates.

SAMPLE GRADATIONAL SENTENCES

(1) "Will you also come tomorrow?"
A. M: *Kimi mo asu kuru ka?*
    F: *Anta mo ashita kuru?*
B. F: *Anata mo ashita irassharu?*
C. *Anata mo ashita kimasu ka?*
D. *LN-san mo ashita koraremasu ka?*
E. *LN-san mo ashita irasshaimasu ka?*
F. *LN-san/Sensei mo ashita irasshaimasen ka?*
G. *LN-san/Sensei mo ashita oide ni narimasu ka?*
H. *LN-san/Sensei mo ashita oide ni narimasen ka?*
I. *LN-san/Sensei mo ashita oide kudasaimasu ka?*
J. *LN-san/Sensei mo ashita oide kudasaimasen ka?*
K. *LN-san/Sensei ni mo ashita oide itadakemasu ka?*
L. *LN-san/Sensei ni mo ashita oide itadakemasen ka?*
M. *LN-san/Sensei mo ashita oide kudasaimasen deshoo ka?*
N. *LN-san/Sensei ni mo myoonichi oide itadakemasen deshoo ka?*

General Observations. When one examines this list, which is by no means exhaustive, one can make a number of observations that apply to English also. For instance, the more polite expressions tend to be longer ("Pass me the salt!"; "May I have the salt, please?"; "Do you mind passing me the salt?"); the negative question tends to be more polite with a stronger meaning, having the connotation of begging or urging ("Won't you pass me the salt, please?"); and the non-definitive way of asking with *deshoo* tends to be more polite ("Would you mind" vs. "Do you mind"). These appear to be sociolinguistic universals.

The Four Levels. In the case of the above 14 gradations (15 sentences), we can divide them into the four major level categories as follows:

N: A - B
P-0: C
P-1: D - H
P-2: I - N

The line between the *da* style of N and the *desu/-masu* style of P is easy to draw. The line between P-1 and P-2, however, is harder to draw, but one might draw it between H and I. Expressions I to N, which contain donatory verbs, have the extra connotation that the speaker would consider it a personal favor to have the addressee come to the function the next day, and thus are very polite.

Politeness Gradation. Let us examine the progression in greater detail. One immediately notices that at the N level men and women speak differently, and that there are two gradations for women. We will see more examples of this soon. As for the progression to greater politeness in this short sentence, the only observable changes are in the address term "you," the verb "come," and the word "tomorrow." The sentence structure changes only in K, L, and N, where, instead of "you," the omitted "I" is the grammatical subject.

The word "**you**" (*anata*, *kimi*, *LN-san/Sensei*) could have been omitted in all the Japanese sentences if the question did not contain the meaning "also." *Anata* having a very narrow usage, it is soon replaced by last name plus *-san*, or title, when appropriate. (*Sensei* in the sample sentences represents "title.") Men have *kimi* available at the N level. How one should address one's speaking partner is discussed in greater detail in Chapter 5.

The most noteworthy aspect in this progression to greater politeness is seen in the **verb phrase**. At the N level, one can use the neutral term *kuru*, although a woman can use the exalting term *irassharu* in N, as illustrated in Sentence B. Supposedly this is to express respect for the addressee, but more likely it is in her upbringing to use such expressions even to an intimate friend, an index of refinement. In Sentence C the neutral verb *kuru* is simply put in the *-masu* form, making it a P-level sentence without showing any special respect for the addressee. Such a sentence may be uttered by a senior to a junior, when the senior is a person who prefers not to use N in addressing his subordinates. Generally at the P levels, one uses exalting verbs for the addressee. *Kuru*, being a verb of high frequency, has a number of exalting substitutes as we can see, varying in the degree of politeness.

We also see a progression of change in the word "**tomorrow**" from the colloquial *asu* to the neutral *ashita* and finally to the formal *myoonichi*.

MORE EXAMPLE SENTENCES

Let us look at some more sentences representing the four levels. Instead of all possible gradations, only representative expressions of the four levels are presented. When the topic of conversation has nothing to do with the addressee nor the speaker, such as the weather, a P-2-level sentence is not always possible. The following level-marking system will be used. Letters in the parentheses indicate the sentence(s) from the set of 15 sentences in (1) that are classified into that particular level.

N: M: Informal male speech (A: M)

F: Informal female speech (A: F)

F+: Informal female speech showing respect to the addressee (B)

P-0: Lowest P-level speech showing no special respect to the addressee. Used in speaking to a complete stranger, to a lower status person politely, and by men to a non-intimate equal (C)

P-1: The minimum essential level of politeness in speaking to a person of higher status, an out-group member, and by women to a non-intimate equal (D to H)

P-2: Ultra-polite level (I to N)

Since P-1 is the minimum essential level of politeness expected in most situations, this book will focus on the P-1 level. All P-1 sentences in the examples will be highlighted. The N-level and P-2-level sentences are supplied for passive comprehension, though they may be used for advanced study if desired.

(2) "That is pretty."
N: M: *Soryaa (=sore wa) kirei da.*
F: *Sore kirei da wa.*
P-0: *Sore wa kirei desu.*
P-2: *Sore wa kirei de gozaimasu.*

(3) "The next train departs at 10:30."
N:M: *Tsugi no ressha wa juuji-han ni deru yo/zo.*
F: *Tsugi no ressha wa juuji-han ni deru wa (yo).*
P-0: *Tsugi no ressha wa juuji-han ni demasu.*
P-2: *Tsugi no ressha wa juuji-han hatsu de gozaimasu ga . . .*

(4) "Did **YOU** go?"
N:M: *Kimi itta ka(i)?*
F: *Anta itta (no)?*
F+: *Anata irasshatta (no)?*
P-0: *Anata wa ikimashita ka?*

P-1: *LN-san/Sensei wa irasshaimashita ka?*
P-2: *LN-san/Sensei wa oide ni nararemashita ka?*

(5) "I am going."
   N: M: *Boku iku.*
      F: *(W)atashi iku wa.*
   P-0: *Watashi wa ikimasu.*
   P-1: *Watakushi wa mairimasu.*
   P-2: *Watakushi wa mairasete itadakimasu ga . . .*

(6) "Do you know that person?"
   N: M: *(Kimi) aitsu shitteru ka(i)?*
      F: *(Anta) ano hito shitteru?*
     F+: *(Anata) ano kata gozonji?*
   P-0: *Ano hito o shitte imasu ka?*
   P-1: *Ano kata o gozonji desu ka?*
   P-2: *Ano kata o gozonji de irasshaimasu ka?*

(7) "Did you see that movie?"
   N: M: *Ano eiga mita ka(i)?*
      F: *Ano eiga mita?*
     F+: *Ano eiga goran ni natta?*
   P-0: *Ano eiga mimashita ka?*
   P-1: *Ano eiga o goran ni narimashita ka?*
   P-2: *Ano eiga o goran ni nararemashita ka?*

(8) "Where is the post office?"
   N: M: *Yuubinkyoku doko da?*
      F: *Yuubinkyoku doko (na no)?*
   P-0: *Yuubinkyoku wa doko desu ka?*
   P-1: *Yuubinkyoku wa dochira deshoo ka?*
   P-2: *Yuubinkyoku wa dochira de gozaimasu ka?*

(9) "I read the book you wrote, it was interesting."
   N: M: *Kimi no kaita hon yonda ga, omoshirokatta.*
      F: *Anata no kaita hon yonda kedo, omoshirokatta wa.*

F+: *Anata no okaki ni natta hon yomasete itadaita kedo, omoshirokatta wa.*

P-0: *Anata no kaita hon yomimashita ga, omoshirokatta desu.*

P-1: **LN-san/Sensei no kakareta/okaki ni natta gohon (o) kyoomibukaku yomimashita.**

P-2: *(LN-san/Sensei no) Okaki ni natta gohon o yomasete itadakimashita ga, taihen benkyoo ni narimashita.*

Sentences without "You" or "I." Upon examination of these eight sets, it becomes immediately obvious that sentences having nothing to do with "you" or "I," such as (2), (3), and (8), are far less complex. One need not bother with exalting terms for "you," nor humbling terms for "I," hence there are not as many polite versions of the statement: F+ is missing in all of these, and P-2 only appears in (8). When "I" or "you" is involved, there are usually two gradations within N for women, although the F+ version is heard less frequently among the younger generation today. The reason there is no F+ for (5) is that the humbling term *mairu* is never used as the sentence-final verb in the plain form.

Male and Female Speech. The difference between male and female speech evident at the N level disappears at the P levels. The male-female difference in P-level speech is that women generally speak more politely, that is, one gradation or so higher, than men, as pointed out in the explanation of P-0 and P-1.

"I" and "You." The progressive change from N to P-2 in the first person pronoun "I" is evident in (5), and that of the second person reference term "you" in (4) and (9).

Formality. The increase in formality with politeness also leads to fuller sentences where post-position particles are not omitted. Refined expressions replace neutral ones at the P-1 or P-2 level, such as *kata* for *hito* in (6), and *dochira* for *doko* in (8).

Less Definite, More Polite. It is also generally more polite to make the statement less definitive or exact. Thus, as shown in (8), it is more polite to say *"doko deshoo ka?"* (Where might it be?) than *"doko desu ka?"* (Where is it?). The P-2-level sentences in (3) and (5) are incomplete, ending in *"ga . . . ,"* which makes the statement less definitive, and thus more polite.

Double Exaltation. (4) and (7) have *ni nararemashita* at the P-2 level. Most Japanese grammarians object to this type of "double *sonkei-go*" construction. *ni naru* is an exalting verb, and to apply the exalting infix *-are* to *naru* results in double exaltation. However, regardless of what the grammarians say, the form *nararemasu* is frequently heard in P-2-level speech.

Use of *sasete itadaku*. At the P-2 level, the donatory verb expression *-(s)asete itadaku* is used to describe the speaker's action. In (9) the first half of the P-2 sentence translates to "Assuming on your permission, I read the book you wrote." This is at an extremely high level of politeness, discussed in greater detail in Chapter 6.

Exaltation First, Humbling Second. Sentences at the P-1 and P-2 levels make use of exalting and humbling verbs (see next chapter). Exalting verbs must be used for all actions of the addressee, but not every action of the speaker needs to be expressed by a humbling verb. In (9) we note that the exalting verb for "write" appears at a lower level (P-1) than the humbling expression for "read" (P-2). The reason is that there are more exalting terms available than there are humbling terms.

Embedded Sentences. What distinguishes P-level sentences from N-level sentences is the verb ending at the very end of the sentence. It is therefore not necessary to use the P or *desu/-masu*-style ending in a sentence embedded in another sentence, such as one used to modify a noun. Note that in (9), even at the P-2 level, *go-hon* is modified by *okaki ni natta* and not *okaki ni narimashita*.

One normally does not say *Sensei ga irasshaimashita toki* or *oide ni narimashita toki*, but simply *Sensei ga irasshatta toki* or *oide ni natta toki*. Only occasionally, some who try to be extra polite at P-2 use the P-level verb ending in embedded sentences.

Notes about Culture

COMPLIMENTS

Complimenting is part of maintaining a smooth relationship. Sentence (9) is an example of a compliment. The Japanese, who constantly exchange compliments, are not accustomed to frank and honest opinions, and thus are extremely sensitive to any sort of criticism. Unless one wants to terminate the relationship, one must suppress criticisms of any kind in relation to a *meue* (senior) person. Even a positive opinion from a *meshita* (junior), such as "Your lecture was great" can be taken as an insult, because it is interpreted as the *meshita* person putting himself above the *meue* person in making such a judgment.

The difference between the P-1 and P-2 levels in (9) is therefore one of content. The P-1 sentence translates to "I read the book you wrote with great interest," while the P-2 sentence translates to "Assuming on your permission, I read the book you wrote, and I learned a great deal from it." To say *omoshiroo gozaimashita* in the *gozaimasu* style would be grammatically acceptable, but not culturally. In a statement addressed to a higher-status person, it is presumptuous to say "I found it interesting," (unless it is a murder mystery), for one should not be judgmental of the work or lecture of someone higher in status. One must put oneself beneath him, and say his book, lecture or work, was very instructive, stimulating, or the like.

MALE AND FEMALE SPEECH

We have already observed some differences in male and female speech. The differences are most pronounced at the N level of speech. Before a summary review of the differences, a brief discussion on male speech appears to be in order.

It was mentioned before that a non-student foreigner has little need for N-level speech when first arriving in Japan as it takes time to develop intimate friends with whom mutual N will be exchanged. Whether with friends in school or colleagues at work, it is easy enough to learn the N level of speech by observation and imitation.

There is, however, another situation for male speakers in which N-level speech enters into the picture. You will remember that in a hierarchical relationship, men tend to speak downwards in N, while women tend to use P-0. In speaking to waiters, waitresses, and taxi drivers too, men tend to use N while women use P-0. Unlike when speaking to individuals of higher status, the individual speaker is essentially free to choose the level of speech when speaking to lower-status persons. To the Japanese male, however, speaking downwards in N is more "macho." In placing an order at a coffee shop or restaurant, he may just say, *Koohii kure*, or *Boku wa tempura*, instead of *Koohii o kudasai*, or *Boku wa tempura ni shimasu*. A man who speaks more politely than necessary may be perceived as being feminine by some. I know, however, a distinguished professor at Tokyo University who spoke at the ultra-polite level even to the taxi driver. Yet, because of his dignified posture, in no way did he come across as being feminine.

Although the N-level of speech is not the focus of our attention in this book, the sample sentences at different levels in the following chapters will give ample examples of male and female speech. The essential differences are listed below.

1. Self-reference term at the N level (See Chapter 5)
   M: *boku, ore*
   F: *watashi, atashi*

2. Address and second person reference term at the N-level
   (See Chapter 5)
   M: LN/FN-*kun*
   F: LN/FN-*san*

3. Sentence particles, mainly at the N-level
   M: *yo, zo, ze, na*
   F: *yo, wa, no, ne*

4. The use of *o-* prefix for common nouns by women (See Chapter 4)

5. Level of speech: Women tend to use more respect (exalting and humbling) terms than men, making the level of speech slightly higher than that of men in similar circumstances. (See Chapter 4)

6. The use of N-level speech downwards: Men tend to use N in speaking to any lower-status person while women generally do so only to those distinctly lower in status, such as to children, students, and domestic servants. The emerging number of women executives, however, may gradually change the established pattern of female speech.

Summary

As we have seen from the examples in this chapter, the P-2 level of politeness requires the use of formal and refined words in addition to exalting and humbling expressions. Cultural considerations also come into play in some cases. The following chapters are devoted to detailed explanations of the elements of politeness gradation presented in this chapter. Your goal is to master at least the P-1 level of politeness in each element. In Chapter 7, we will bring the elements together for a summary of levels. When one is depending on the addressee's help or cooperation, the use of polite speech with appropriate exalting terms is essential. It may mean the difference between *yes* or *no* in obtaining the assistance one seeks.

4. Expressing Respect: Exalting and Humbling Words

The essential rule in Japanese conversational speech is to show respect to the addressee. This generally applies to the polite P level of speech. At the N level, as we have seen, the addressee is treated as an intimate (family member, close friend, etc.) or as a lower-status person and terms of respect tend to be dispensed with.

As we have also seen, the idea of showing respect to the addresee is governed by two rules. The most important general rule to remember is **the in-group/out-group principle. In interactions across groups, all in-group members are humbled, and all out-group members, that is the addressee's group members, are exalted regardless of age or status**. In other words, members of the addressee's group are treated as if all of them have higher status, while all members of the speaker's group are treated as if they are of lower status. **In interactions among members within the same group, however, the status hierarchy is strictly observed.** This is particularly important in a work setting.

This **respect to the addressee is shown by exalting the addressee while at the same time humbling oneself**, thereby increasing the vertical distance between the speaker and the addressee. **The exalting terms (*sonkei-go*) apply to the addressee (and to a third person for whom respect is shown), while the humbling terms (*kenjoo-go*) to the speaker, and they go hand in hand. It should be remembered that "addressee" means not only "you," but includes people and things that belong to "you," such as members of "your" family, "your" group and "your" home, books, etc., while "speaker" means not only "I," but also members of "my" family, "my" group, and "my" possessions.

Among exalting and humbling terms, the most important are verbs, covered in this chapter, and address/reference terms, in the next chapter. Verbs can be especially difficult; some beginning students of Japanese wrongly associate exalting verbs with polite speech, and humbling verbs with nonpolite speech. They could not be more wrong. For one thing, in nonpolite speech, one usually dispenses with humbling as well as exalting verbs. For another, the exalting verb and the humbling verb can appear in the same sentence, such as in "If *you go* (exalting), *I will go* (humbling) too" (*Oide ni naru no deshitara, watakushi mo mairimasu*).

There are exalting and humbling words and morphemes in the various parts of speech. Some are lexical items replacing their neutral equivalents. Others are produced grammatically. We will discuss the verbs first, and then cover common nouns. Adjectives and adverbs are discussed under other parts of speech at the end of the chapter. For study methods, see summary sections.

Verbs

LEXICAL SUBSTITUTION

Verbs that are used at high frequencies tend to have exalting and humbling substitutes to replace the neutral verbs. Since the exalting ones are to be used in reference to "you," the addressee, and the humbling ones for "I," the speaker, mixing up the exalting and humbling verbs can have comical if not insulting consequences. The essential ones are listed in Chart 1.

A glance at Chart 1 makes it obvious that lexical substitution of exalting and humbling verbs for the neutral ones are by no means symmetrical.

Chart 1: Exalting and Humbling Verbs: Lexical Substitutes

English	Neutral	Exalting	Humbling
to do	*suru*	*nasaru*	*itasu*
to be at a place	*iru*	*irassharu* *o-ide ni naru*	*oru*
to go	*iku*	*irassharu* *o-ide ni naru*	*mairu*
to come	*kuru*	*irassharu* *o-ide ni naru* *o-mie ni naru*	*mairu*
to say	*iu*	*ossharu*	*moosu* *mooshiageru*
to know	*shitte iru*	*go-zonji de irassharu*	*zonjite oru*
to look at	*miru*	*goran ni naru*	*haiken suru*
to go to bed	*neru*	*o-yasumi ni naru*	—
to die	*shinu*	*o-nakunari ni naru*	—
to put on (clothes)	*kiru*	(*o-meshi ni naru*)[1]	—
to eat	*taberu*	*meshiagaru* *o-agari ni naru*	*itadaku*
to drink	*nomu*	*meshiagaru* *o-agari ni naru*	*itadaku*
to inquire	*kiku* *tazuneru*	—	*ukagau*
to visit	*tazuneru*	—	*ukagau*
to borrow	*kariru*	—	*haishaku suru*
to meet	*au*	—	*o-me ni kakaru*

[1] Not used much in today's Japanese

GRAMMATICAL DEVICES

For verbs that do not have lexical substitutes, the exalting and humbling forms are produced grammatically. There are essentially two ways to create exalting forms: *o-___ ni naru* and *are-/-rare-*; but only one way to create the humbling form: *o-___ suru*, which has restricted usage. These grammatical devices can be applied also to some of the neutral verbs that have lexical substitutes as can be seen in Charts 2 and 4.

Exalting

o-___ ni naru. The *o-* + Verb Stem + *ni naru* form is easy to make. Take the verb in its *-masu* form, such as *kakimasu*, drop the *masu,* and what you have left is the verb stem (stem of the vowel-ending weak verb, or stem + *i* of the consonant-ending strong verb, to be exact). Attach the prefix *o-* to the stem, and let *ni naru* follow the stem, and you have the exalting form of the verb. The verbs with lexical substitutes in Chart 1 include a number of exalting verbs that are similar in form, but notice that the verb stem following *o-* is a lexical substitute, having no resemblance to the neutral verb.

In the *o-___ ni naru* construction, *naru* becomes the main verb and conjugates like any other verb. One can say *o-yomi ni naremasu* with the meaning "is able to read," *o-yomi ni naritai no desu ka*, "Do you want to read?" and so on.

-are-/-rare-. Compared with the *o-___ ni naru* form, the *-are-/-rare-* form is slightly more cumbersome to produce. Attach *-are-* to the consonant-ending root of a verb, *-rare-* to the vowel-ending root of a verb. They come between the root and the final verb ending.

As can be seen in Chart 3, the formation of the exalting form by grammatical devices is quite regular for verbs that do not have lexical substitutes. Those that have lexical substitutes tend to be verbs with one-syllable stems used at high frequencies. They cannot be made into the *o-___ ni naru* form of exaltation. It is important that the lexical substitutes be memorized for everyday use.

Women tend to prefer the *o-___ ni naru* form while men tend to use the *-rare/-are-* form. The *-are-/-rare-* form of exaltation is considered to be rather formal, and thus is used in speeches, lectures, and journalistic writing.

Chart 2: Verbs with Lexical Substitutes for Exaltation

English	Neutral	Substitutes	Grammatically Produced Forms	
			o-__ ni naru	*-are-/-rare-*
to do	*suru*	*nasaru*	—	*s-are-ru*
to be at a place	*iru*	*irassharu* *o-ide ni naru*	—	*i-rare-ru*[2]
to go	*iku*	*irassharu* *o-ide ni naru*	—	*ik-are-ru*
to come	*kuru*	*irassharu* *o-ide ni naru* *o-mie ni naru*	—	*ko-rare-ru*
to say	*iu*	*ossharu*	—	*iw-are-ru*
to know	*shitte-iru*	*gozonji de irassharu*	*gozonji de* —	*ir-are-ru*
to look at	*miru*	*goran ni naru*	—	*mi-rare-ru*
to go to bed	*neru*	*o-yasumi ni naru*	—	*ne-rare-ru*
to die	*shinu*	*o-nakunari ni naru*	—	*nakunara-re-ru*
to put on (clothes)	*kiru*	*(o-meshi ni naru)*	—	*ki-rare-ru*
to eat	*taberu*	*meshiagaru* *o-agari ni naru*	—	*tabe-rare-ru*
to drink	*nomu*	*meshiagaru* *o-agari ni naru*	*o-nomi ni naru*	*nom-are-ru*

[2] Many people today use *or-are-ru* as an exalting verb instead of *i-rare-ru*. Having been formed from the humbling verb *oru*, it is not exactly correct, although the common usage is leading to its acceptability.

A verb with **the passive *-are-/-rare-*** and one with the exalting *-are-/-rare-* are exactly the same in shape. The difference in meaning can be derived only from the sentence structure, and—when the understood noun phrase is omitted—from context, as shown below.

Passive: *(Watashi wa) Tanaka-san **ni** soo iw-are-mashita.*
"I was subjected to Tanaka-san saying so (something negative)."

Exalting: *Tanaka-san **wa** soo iw-are-mashita.*
=Tanaka-san wa soo osshaimashita.
"Tanaka-san said so."

o-___ desu. It should be added that there is a third way to exalt a verb. It is the *o-___ desu* form, where *ni naru* is replaced by *desu*, such as *o-dekake desu* instead of *o-dekake ni narimasu* (to depart/leave). This form, however, has a rather restricted usage. It is used generally in reference to a present or future time period, and mainly in questions addressed to a second person or in speaking about a third person. Not all verbs can be put in this form either. Hence it is mentioned here only for the purpose of passive comprehension.

Chart 3: Sample Verbs without Exalting Lexical Substitutes

English	Neutral	Grammatically Produced Forms	
		o-___ ni naru	*-are/-rare*
to ask/listen	*kiku*	*o-kiki ni naru*	*kik-are-ru*
to ask/visit	*tazuneru*	*o-tazune ni naru*	*tazune-rare-ru*
to borrow	*kariru*	*o-kari ni naru*	*kari-rare-ru*
to meet	*au*	*o-ai ni naru*	*aw-are-ru*
to read	*yomu*	*o-yomi ni naru*	*yom-are-ru*
to write	*kaku*	*o-kaki ni naru*	*kak-are-ru*
to feel	*omou*	*o-omoi ni naru*	*omow-are-ru*
to take	*toru*	*o-tori ni naru*	*tor-are-ru*
to rejoice	*yorokobu*	*o-yorokobi ni naru*	*yorokob-are-ru*
to get up	*okiru*	*o-oki ni naru*	*oki-rare-ru*
to think	*kangaeru*	*o-kangae ni naru*	*kangae-rare-ru*
to obtain	*eru*	—	*e-rare-ru*

Humbling

The humbling verbs with lexical substitutes have already been introduced. As was mentioned, grammatically there is only one way to produce humbling verbs from neutral ones: the *o-___ suru* form. **While one uses the exalting form for every verb phrase that refers to the addressee's (and his in-group member's) action, one need not use a humbling form for all of one's own actions.** The reason will soon become clear.

o-___ suru. The humbling *o-___ suru* is formed in a similar manner to the exalting *o-___ ni naru* form.

A number of verbs that have lexical substitutes for humbling have grammatical alternates also, as was the case for exaltation.

Restricted Use of Humbling Verbs. Humbling verbs that consist of **lexical substitutes** are used indiscriminately as long as the action refers to oneself, namely the speaker or in-group members of the speaker. In contrast to the lexical substitutes, **humbling verbs produced by grammatical means** generally have the connotation that the action is carried out on behalf of the addressee or members of the addressee's group, or a third person who is the topic. Consequently, it has a rather restricted usage. It is for this reason that not every verb can be put in this form.

To give an example, *o-kaki suru,* or the sentence *o-kaki shimasu,* does not simply mean "I will write," but rather "I will write for you." Suppose two people not very intimate, speaking in mutual P, have been discussing a book, and one asks the other whether he/she has read it.

A: *Ano hon o o-yomi ni narimashita ka*
   "Did you read that book?"
B: *Ee, yomimashita.*
   "Yes, I did."

Note that while *yomu* is in the exalting form *o-yomi ni narimashita* in the question, the answer referring to the speaker's action is not in the humbling form. If the humbling form were used as in,

Chart 4: Verbs with Lexical Substitutes for Humbling

English	Neutral	Substitute	Grammatically Produced Form *o-___ suru*
to do	*suru*	*itasu*	—
to be at a place	*iru*	*oru*	—
to go	*iku*	*mairu*	—
to come	*kuru*	*mairu*	—
to say	*iu*	*moosu* *mooshiageru*	—
to know	*shitte iru*	*zonjite oru*	—
to look at	*miru*	*haiken suru*	—
to eat	*taberu*	*itadaku*	—
to drink	*nomu*	*itadaku*	—
to inquire	*kiku*	*ukagau*	*o-kiki suru* *o-ukagai suru*
to visit/inquire	*tazuneru*	*ukagau*	*o-tazune suru* *o-ukagai suru*
to borrow	*kariru*	*haishaku suru*	*o-kari suru*
to meet	*au*	*o-me ni kakaru*	*o-ai suru*

Chart 5: Sample Verbs without Humbling Lexical Substitutes

English	Neutral	Grammatically Produced Form *o-___ suru*
to read	*yomu*	*o-yomi suru*
to write	*kaku*	*o-kaki suru*
to feel/think	*omou*	—
to rejoice	*yorokobu*	*o-yorokobi suru*
to get up	*okiru*	—
to think	*kangaeru*	—

B: *Ee, o-yomi shimashita.*
    "Yes, I read it for you (or a member of your group)."

it would be an answer to a question such as,

A: *Ano hon o Hanako ni yonde kuremashita ka?*
    "Did you read that book for my Hanako?"

Because of this extra connotation of the *o-___ suru* form, it can usually be replaced with the *___-te ageru* form (discussed in the section on Donatory Verbs in Chapter 6). Thus *o-yomi suru* has the same meaning as *yonde ageru* or *yonde sashiageru.*

It should also be noted that *suru* has the humbling substitute word *itasu*, making it possible to increase the degree of humbling, and thus politeness, from *o-yomi shimashita* to *o-yomi itashimashita.*

COMPOUND VERB PHRASES

When two verbs are joined to form a compound verb phrase, the first verb is a gerund in *-te* form and the second verb functions grammatically as the main verb. The gerund remains intact, and the second verb undergoes grammatical changes to indicate tense and aspect, as well as exaltation and humility.

Verbs such as *iru*, *iku*, and *kuru*, used frequently as the second verb in compound verb phrases, have all the lexical substitutes as well as the grammatically produced equivalents of exaltation and humbling available. Examples of exalting and humbling are given in Chart 6.

The examples in Chart 6 should remind us of the difference in usage of the exalting verbs and the humbling verbs. In contrast to the broad applicability of exaltation, the use of humbling is extremely limited. When there are lexical substitutes for the main verb, there are no problems. The grammatically formed *o-___ suru* form, however, cannot be used except for the special meaning of "doing for you." Hence *motte kaeru* cannot be put in the *o-___ suru* form. In the context "I will take it to my home for you," one

Chart 6: Compound Verb Phrases

Neutral (English)	Exalting	Humbling
yonde iru (to be reading)	*yonde irassharu* *yonde o-ide ni naru* *yonde i-rare-ru*	*yonde oru*
katte iku (to buy on the way)	*katte irassharu* *katte o-ide ni naru* *katte ik-are-ru*	*katte mairu*
katte kuru (to go buy and come back)	*katte irassharu* *katte o-ide ni naru* *katte ko-rare-ru*	*katte mairu*
motte kaeru (to take it home)	*motte o-kaeri ni naru* *motte kaer-are-ru*	—
Shimete oku (to keep it closed)	*shimete o-oki ni naru* *shimete ok-are-ru*	*(shimete o-oki suru)*[3]
wasurete shimau (to end up forgetting)	*wasurete o-shimai ni naru* — *wasurete shimaw-are-ru*	—

[3] Shimete o-oki suru means "I will keep it closed for you" or "at your request."

would have to say *Motte kaette (sashi)agemashoo*, enlisting the help of a donatory verb. The last, "to end up forgetting," obviously cannot be put in a humble expression.

SUMMARY OF EXALTING AND HUMBLING VERBS

The fact that exalting expressions are used for the addressee, and humbling expressions for the speaker, means that the verb phrase used in a question directed to the addressee is not repeated in the answer.

(1) A: "Did you go to last week's alumni reunion?"
*Senshuu no doosookai ni **oide ni narimashita** ka?*

B: "Unfortunately I was busy and couldn't go."
Zannen nagara isogashikute **mairemasen** *deshita.*

(2) A: "Is your father well?"
Otoo-sama wa o-genki de **irasshaimasu** *ka?*
B: "Thank you. He's been fine since he had the surgery."
Okagesama de shujutsu shite kara wa zutto genki de **orimasu**.

On the other hand, if the question does not relate to the addressee, the same verb phrase can be used in the answer.

(3) A: "I wonder if Prof. Watanabe is already back (= has already returned) from America."
Watanabe Sensei wa moo Amerika kara kaette **irasshatta** *n deshoo ka?*
B: "I think he is already back."
Moo kaette **irasshatta** *n da to omoimasu.*

(4) A: "How does one say 'gozen, gogo' in English?"
Eigo de gozen, gogo tte doo iimasu ka?
B: "One says 'a.m., p.m.'"
Ee emu, pii emu tte **iimasu**.

While all that has been presented above may look rather troublesome to master, once you memorize the lexical substitutes to express exaltation and humbling in Chart 1, the rest is not that complicated. You may want to use consistently one of the two ways of grammatically forming exalting verbs for production, and reserve the other for comprehension only. Men might choose the *-are-/-rare-* form. As for humbling verbs, because the grammatically produced version has limited usage, its mastery may be put off until you have the exalting verbs under control. Obviously the appropriate use of exalting verbs is more important than the humbling verbs, except those in Chart 1, which have high frequency usage.

Nouns

Nouns are made honorific by using the prefix *o-* or *go-*. Nouns referring to persons often have the suffix *-san*. The latter case is discussed in the next chapter on address and reference terms. Here we will discuss mainly non-person nouns.

NOUNS TO SHOW RESPECT TO THE ADDRESSEE

The honorific prefix *o-* or *go-*, or sometimes *on-*, is attached to things belonging or related to the person the speaker shows **respect** to, namely the addressee, members of the addressee's group, or a third person who is not a member of the speaker's group. The three prefixes have the same meaning, and which of the three is used with a particular noun depends partly on customary use, and partly on whether the noun is a Chinese compound or not.

go-. The *go-* prefix is attached to Chinese compounds (or *on*-reading nouns) to create exalting nouns. One exception to this is the word *go-han*, in women's everyday speech, referring to "cooked rice" or "meal." Men use the word *meshi*, the *kun* reading of the kanji *han* of *go-han*, at the N-level.

o-. Japanese-origin nouns (*Yamato kotoba*, or nouns with *kun* reading) take the *o-* prefix. However, there are a large number of Chinese compounds used so frequently in daily life as not to be perceived as words of Chinese origin and take the *o-* prefix rather than the *go-* prefix.

on-. The third variant *on-* is used with only a handful of nouns, and never used in speech, but only in writing. Nouns with the *on-* prefix are used in reference to the addressee only.

Japanese grammarians usually classify the use of these prefixes according to one of three categories: for exaltation; for humbling; and for refinement. Such a grammatical classification appears to be unnecessary for practical application. In the following charts, nouns with appropriate prefixes will be presented in two categories: Chart 7 lists those used specifically to show **respect** to the addressee, a member of the addressee's group, or a third person who is not an in-group member of the speaker; and Chart 8 lists those used in everyday speech for **refinement** by women, and only at the P-1 level by men.

Chart 7: Nouns with Honorific Prefix to Show Respect [4]

Prefix	Noun	English
go-:	go-iken	"your opinion"
	go-kansoo	"your feeling"
	go-kiboo	"your desire"
	go-shinpai	"your concern/worry"
	go-juusho	"your address"
	go-senmon	"your specialty"
	go-shusseki	"your attendance (at a meeting)"
	go-shukkin	"your attendance (at office)"
	go-jishin	"yourself"
	go-intai	"your retirement"
	go-byooki	"your illness"
	go-hon	"your book"
o-:	o-kotoba	"your word, say"
	o-kangae	"your idea"
	o-namae	"your name"
	o-sumai	"your residence"
	o-umare	"your birth (place or date)"
	o-kuni	"your native country or region"
	o-toshi	"your age"
	o-tsumori	"your intention"
	o-hima	"your free time"
	o-jikan	"your time"
	o-tegami	"your letter" or "my letter to you"
	o-henji	"your answer" or "my answer to you"

Prefix	Noun	English
	o-denwa	"your telephone call" or "my call to you"
	o-shashin	"your photograph"
	o-genki	"your good health"
	o-rusu	"your absence from home"
	o-suki	"your fondness"
	o-kirai	"your dislike"
	o-ki ni iri	"your favorite"
on-:	on-mi	"your body (health)"
	on-rei	"gratitude to you
	on-chi	"your locale"
	on-sha	"your company"
	on-shi	"the magazine you publish"

⁴ This list is not exhaustive.

These nouns may be found in the following P-1 sentences:

(5) "May I have your opinion on this issue?"
*Kono koto ni tsuite no **go-iken** o o-ukagai shitai n desu ga* . . .

(6) "I am sorry to have caused you worries."
***Go-shinpai** (o) o-kake shite mooshiwake arimasen deshita.*

(7) "Will you attend the next meeting? (Are you willing to do us the favor of attending the next meeting?)"
*Tsugi no kaigoo ni **go-shusseki** itadakemasu ka?*

(8) "Where do you live?"
***O-sumai** wa dochira desu ka?*

(9) "What (part of the) country does your daughter-in-law come from?"
*O-yome-san wa **o-kuni** wa dochira desu ka?*

(10) "I called you yesterday, but you were not home, so . . ."
*Kinoo **o-denwa** shimashita ga, **o-rusu** de irasshaimashita node . . .*

(11) "Please do come when you have time."
***O-hima** no toki wa zehi oide kudasai.*

(12)"I saw your photograph. It came out really well."
***O-shashin** (o) haiken shimashita ga, hontoo ni yoku torete imasu ne.* (if addressee took a picture of someone or something)
***O-shashin** (o) haiken shimashita ga, hontoo ni yoku torete irasshaimasu ne.* (if addressee is in the photograph)

(13)"I am extremely sorry that my answer to your letter is so late."
***O-tegami** e no **o-henji** ga osoku natte, mooshiwake arimasen.*

(14) "I express my gratitude to you." (in letters only)
***On-rei** mooshiagemasu.*

(15)"Please take care of yourself (your health)." (mostly in letters)
***On-mi** go-taisetsu ni nasatte kudasaimase.*

These nouns with the *o-* and *go-* prefixes can also be used in reference to a third person when the speaker wants to show respect for him, as follows:

(16)"Prof. Watanabe is sick."
*Watanabe Sensei wa **go-byooki** desu.*

NOUNS IN EVERYDAY FEMALE SPEECH FOR REFINEMENT

Women tend to attach the *o-* prefix to commonly used nouns in everyday speech at both the P and N levels, regardless of whether it has to do with the addressee or not. In other words, the honorific prefixes are used for **refinement**, as these nouns without

Chart 8: Nouns with Honorific Prefix for Refinement[5]

Prefix	Category	Noun	English
go-:		go-han	cooked rice, meal
o-:	Annual events:	o-shoogatsu	New Year
		o-hinamatsuri	Girl's Day (March 3)
		o-bon	The Buddhist All Souls' Day
		o-matsuri	festival
	Food items:	o-cha	tea
		o-kome	rice (uncooked)
		o-yasai	vegetables
		o-negi	green onions
		o-daikon	turnip
		o-niku	meat
		o-sakana	fish
		o-kashi	sweets
		o-senbei	senbei (rice crackers)
		o-toofu	tofu
		o-tsukemono	pickles
		o-shooyu	soy sauce
		o-sake	rice wine
		o-miso	soybean paste
		o-sushi	sushi
		o-nigiri	rice ball
		o-bentoo	box lunch
		o-ryoori	menu, cooked dishes
		o-shokuji	meal
	Food utensils:	o-hashi	chopsticks
		o-chawan	rice bowl
		o-wan	lacquer soup bowl
	Miscellaneous:	o-yasumi	vacation, time off
		o-tsutome	work, duties
		o-tetsudai	help
		o-tenki	weather
		o-tooban	being on duty
		o-miyage	souvenir gift

[5] Used by women in everyday speech at both N and P levels, but only at P level by men.

the prefix sound too crude otherwise. Men attach the prefix to these nouns mainly in reference to the addressee at the P-1 level and above.

The nouns in Chart 8 are used with the honorific prefix for refinement all the time by women, even at the N level, in contrast to those for respect in Chart 7, which are used only at the P-1 and P-2 levels. Men generally use the nouns in Chart 8 without the *o-* prefix in N-level speech. The list is by no means exhaustive.

There are some nouns that cannot be separated from the prefix *o-*, such as *o-yatsu* (a snack between meals), *o-kazu* (side dishes), *o-mairi* (a visit to the shrine to pray). These will not be listed here as they are found listed with the *o-* in the dictionary. Some women, particularly waitresses, attach the prefix *o-* even to foreign loan words, such as *o-biiru* (beer). Because there are many nouns that are used without the honorific prefix, **it is best to limit the application of *o-* to words you yourself have heard in the *o-* form**.

Other Parts of Speech

Only a limited number of adjectives and adverbs (including the *-ku* form of the adjective) take the *go-* or *o-* prefix, either to express respect for the addressee, or as refinement. The latter use is generally limited to female speech. **The beginning learner of polite speech need to memorize only some patterned greetings and terms regarding the condition of health in which adjectives and adverbs appear with the honorific prefix. There are also important lexical substitutions for frequently used demonstratives, which one should become familiar with.**

All examples below are at the P-1 level, except where indicated otherwise.

ADJECTIVAL AND ADVERBIAL EXPRESSIONS
yukkuri (slowly)
(17) "Please take your time." "Please relax and don't rush."
  Doozo go-yukkuri.

mottomo (reasonable, justifiable)
(18) "That (what you say) makes sense." or "I understand your statement/position."
   *Sore wa **go-mottomo** desu.*

wakai (young)
(19) "My, you *are* young!"
   ***O-wakakute** irasshaimasu nee.*

hayai (quick, soon, early)
(20) "Please eat it soon."
   ***O-hayaku** meshiagatte kudasai.*

samui, atsui (cold, hot)
(21) "It's cold/hot." (Greeting on seeing someone in winter or summer, often followed by *O-kawari arimasen ka?* "How are you?")
   ***O-samuu** gozaimasu.* (P-2)
   ***O-atsuu** gozaimasu.* (P-2)

The greeting *Ohayoo gozaimasu* is in the same form as the above two greetings. Unlike the above two greetings, which can be said at the P-O level *Atsui desu ne* by men and *O-atsui desu ne* by women, *Ohayoo gozaimasu* is a general P-level greeting, without a less polite version. In other words, it should not be considered a *gozaimasu* or P-2 expression. The only less polite expression is *Ohayoo*, which is clearly an N-level greeting to be used only to a lower-status person or an intimate equal.

joozu (skillful, good at)
(22) "You speak English well!"
   *Eigo ga **o-joozu** de irasshaimasu ne.*

genki (healthy)
(23) "Is your son, who is in America, all right?"
   *Amerika no o-botchan wa **o-genki** de irasshaimasu ka?*

joobu (strong, healthy)
(24) "Your father is really healthy and strong, isn't he?"
  *Otoo-sama wa hontoo ni **o-joobu** de irasshaimasu ne.*

Women who are, or want to appear, refined tend to overuse the honorific prefix. However, this trend seems to be dying out among the young, with the exception of salespeople. In speaking to customers, salespeople use a great deal of exalting and humbling terms, including the honorific prefix. The following sales talk is an example for passive comprehension.

o-yasui, o-takai (cheap, expensive)
(25) "This has a low price, and is really a bargain."
  *Kore wa **o-nedan** mo **o-yasui** shi, hontoo ni **o-tokuyoo** de gozaimasu.* (P-2)

DEMONSTRATIVE PRONOUNS: KO-, SO-, A-, DO- WORDS

The *ko-, so-, a-, do-* sets of demonstratives have an exalting or refined set, namely the **kochira, sochira, achira, dochira** set, which is used in P-1 and P-2 by both men and women. This refined set is used in place of the pronouns *kore, sore, are, dore*, place pronouns *koko, soko, asoko, doko*, and the pronouns of direction as well as those indicating "which of the two," *kotchi, sotchi, atchi,* and *dotchi*.

Related to these sets of demonstrative pronouns is the set of demonstrative adverbs meaning "in this/that/what way," *koo, soo, aa, doo*. These are the colloquial way of saying *kono yoo ni, sono yoo ni,* and so on. Only the interrogative *doo* or *dono yoo ni* has the refined substitute: *ikaga*, which appears in (30) below.

Some examples of usage follow. All sentences are P-1 except where otherwise noted.
(26) "This person here is Watanabe Sensei." (in introduction)
  Kochira (= kono **kata**) wa Watanabe Sensei desu.
  cf. "This person here is my wife."
  Kore (= kono **hito**) wa kanai desu.

Chart 9: *ko-*, *so-*, *a-*, *do-* Words

	"this"	"that"	"that in far distance"	interrogative
Pronoun "thing"	*kore*	*sore*	*are*	*dore*
Place pronoun	*koko*	*soko*	*asoko*	*doko*
Pronoun of direction or choice between two	*kotchi*	*sotchi*	*atchi*	*dotchi*
Refined substitutes for all of the above	***kochira***	***sochira***	***achira***	***dochira***
Adverbial "in such a way"	*koo*	*soo*	*aa*	*doo*
Refined substitute for the above	—	—	—	***ikaga***

(27) "How quiet this place is!"
   Kochira *wa o-shizuka de gozaimasu nee.* (P-2)

(28) "The station is in that direction."
   *Eki wa **achira** no hoo desu.*

(29) "How about this one?"
   Kochira *wa **ikaga** desu ka?*

In (26), it should be noted that *kochira* is definitely an exalting term. In referring to an out-group or higher status person, one would use *kochira*, while *kore* is used in referring to an in-group member. It should also be noted that the term "person" has exalting and humble substitutes.

neutral: *hito*
exalting: *kata*
humbling: *mono*

The humbling term *mono* is not used much except by sales representatives, and older people. In (26) cf. *kore* can be replaced by *kono hito*, but not by *kono mono*. *Mono* is used most frequently in business contexts like the following:

(30) "This is who I am." (handing over the business card)
*Koo iu **mono** desu ga . . .*

(31) "Someone from our company will deliver it to you."
*Uchi no **mono** ga o-todoke itashimasu.*

Summary Guide

A step-by-step guide is given below. When you have mastered one step, move on to the next. An effort should be made to reach the minimum essential level of politeness so as not to offend the addressee. The essential steps are listed in bold print. If you plan to live in Japan for a long time, and have Japanese relatives, in-laws, or associates, it is recommended that you not stop at the minimum essential level, but go beyond it.

1. **Memorize the frequently used exalting and humbling verbs in Chart 1.**

2. **Master either the *o-___ ni naru* or *-are-/-rare-* form of producing exalting verbs out of neutral verbs. Men are encouraged to choose the *-are-/-rare-* form.**

3. **Familiarize yourself with the use of honorific prefixes used with nouns for expressing respect to the addressee.**

4. If you are a woman, familiarize yourself with the use of the *o*-prefix for refinement in commonly used nouns. Non-use of the *o*-prefix will result in being perceived as an unsophisticated, crude, masculine woman.

5. Master the last section of this chapter on other parts of speech.

6. As a last step master the *o*-___ *suru* form of humbling verbs, being aware of its restricted use.

5. How to say "YOU" and "I": Address and Reference Terms

The most important aspect of speaking politely in Japanese, aside from the *desu/-masu* sentence ending, is the address term—how to address your speaking partner—and the reference term—how to refer to him or her, namely how to say "you" in sentences. When you call after someone, let's say Prof. Smith, and say, "Prof. Smith, may I speak with you for a moment?" "Prof. Smith" is the address term, and "you" in the sentence is the reference term, in this case a second person pronoun.

It is in addressing someone and in referring to that person in sentences with the equivalent of "you" where *faux pas* with the most serious consequences occur. The foreigner who has learned that the Japanese word for "you" is *anata* tends to put *anata* in every sentence that contains the word "you" or "your" in the equivalent sentence in his first language. The Japanese sentence does not require the grammatical subject or object to be stated when it is understood from the context. As mentioned earlier, the use of *anata* can lead to devastating outcomes, for it means that you consider the addressee to be of lower status than yourself. Strange as it may seem, there is no second person pronoun ("you") that can be comfortably used at the P level of speech in today's Japan.

In a 1982 television program on the Japanese language, there was a roundtable discussion in which TV journalists were asked how they address ordinary people on the street when they survey the reactions of the public to various social and political issues. The journalists were unanimous in expressing their frustrations in searching for appropriate words by which to address or refer to their interviewees. To say to a stranger from whom they want to enlist cooperation, *Anata wa kore ni tsuite doo omoimasu ka?* ("What do you think about this?") would be rude and might turn them off. Some journalists found relief when the potential interviewee was accompanied by children, allowing them to use a kinship term, as in *Otoosan wa kore ni tsuite doo omoimasu ka?* (See "Kinship Terms" below.) A woman in her forties could be addressed *oku-san* (Madam), but otherwise, since they knew neither the name nor the occupation of the addressee, some of the common address terms, such as *sensei*, *shachoo-san* (company president), or *okyaku-san* ("Mr./Ms. Customer"), could not be applied. The fact that professionals engaged in interviewing strangers had no answer to offer the public is indicative of the serious problem even native speakers face in Japan today.

The devaluation of the word *anata* is largely responsible for the interviewer's frustration. At one time in history, second person pronouns like *anata*, *kimi*, *omae*, and *kisama* were exalting words which showed respect, but over the centuries, they lost their respect value and came to be used in addressing lower-status persons with varying degrees of vulgarity. Unfortunately, no new words have come into existence to take their places, causing difficulties at the P levels of speech. At the N level, however, there is little problem.

In Japan the personal pronouns "you" and "I" are not used as much as in Western languages. They tend to be used only for emphasis or contrast. Besides the fact that understood nouns are normally omitted, the use of exalting verbs for "you" and the humbling verbs for "I" makes clear whom one is speaking about. There is no shortage in the variety of first person pronouns for "I." However, because one need not use the word "I" for the reasons given above, its unnecessary use results in giving the impression that the speaker is an ego-centric, boisterous person. Generally, only for emphasis, or when contrasting oneself to someone else, does one use the first person pronoun.

Both the first and second person pronouns are only a small part of reference terms in Japanese. Since the pronoun "you" can be used only at the N level of speech, how to say "you" and how to address a person are rather complicated in Japanese. In this chapter, how to address a person, and how to say "you" and "I" in general situations, will be presented first. The special cases of how to say "you" and "I" within the family, and how to refer to one's own family members and those of the addressee's, as well as how to speak to in-laws, are discussed under "Kinship Terms." How to say "you" and "I" in relation to children is covered in the section "Speaking to Children."

How to Address a Person in General

Unless you come to Japan as a student, all your new relationships with adults will require that you speak at a P level, where the second person pronoun *anata* is taboo.

The general rules will be given first, before plunging into details and exceptions.

1. The most general way to address an adult is by the last name (LN) plus -*san*, except those who are addressed by their titles, and intimate friends, who may be addressed in various ways.

2. In sentences, the word "you" is replaced by whatever address term is used for that particular person. This is a requirement at the P level of speech, and optional at the N level.

Rule 2 will be discussed under the section "How to Say You" after we have first covered the address terms.

TITLES

Most individuals who have titles should be addressed by their titles. Not to do so would be an insult to the addressee, and addressing them by LN-*san* is also inappropriate and is considered presumptuous.

Sensei. An address term with fairly broad applicability is *sensei*. *Sensei* literally means "born earlier" and is translated as "teacher." It is a respectful term used to address and refer to teachers from kindergarten up to university professors, tutors, teachers of private lessons in music, flower arrangement, and so on. In addition, doctors, dentists, and members of the Diet are addressed as *sensei*. They are addressed and referred to as *sensei* not only by their students, pupils, and clients, but also by anybody who comes into contact with them. One can address someone who is an authority on a subject, and for whom one has respect, as *sensei* even if the person is not a teacher. The category of people who may be addressed as *sensei* seems to be rapidly broadening to include one's lawyer, accountant, and in some cases even one's hairdresser! This may very well be a result of the great inconvenience of not having a P-level second person pronoun.

When one addresses a particular *sensei* among many present, the address term is LN-*sensei*.

-choo. Those who are heads of an agency, office, or institution have a title ending in -*choo*, which means "head." These people are usually addressed with the -*choo* title, sometimes followed by -*san*, or by *sensei*. *Sensei* is attached to heads who are professionals normally addressed as *sensei*. However, in addressing a particular person among several with the same title, such as at a mayors' or doctors' conference, the way to address him would be LN + title without -*san* or *sensei*, such as *Murakami-Shichoo* or *Hasegawa-Inchoo*.

The -*choo* title is not to be taken lightly. The rank-conscious Japanese may be insulted if he is treated as one of the many. A letter to the editor in one of the papers in Japan reported of an incident where the wife of a dying patient asked the nurse to try to rouse her husband, since he was responding only to the voices of the doctor and the head nurse by then. She used *anata* to address

Chart 10: Titles for Heads of Organizations and Institutions[6]

Title	Meaning	Address Term
shachoo	president of a company	*Shachoo-san*
shochoo	head of a police station	*Shochoo-san*
shochoo	director of an institute	*Shochoo-san*
	kenkyuujo: research inst.	*Shochoo-sensei*
kaichoo	association president	*Kaichoo(-san)*
kyokuchoo	head of a post office	*Kyokuchoo-san*
shichoo	mayor of a city	*Shichoo-san*
choochoo	mayor of a town	*Choochoo-san*
sonchoo	mayor of a village	*Sonchoo-san*
inchoo	head of a hospital/clinic	*Inchoo-sensei*
ichoo	head physician of a medical division in a hospital	*Ichoo-sensei*
fuchoo	head nurse	*Fuchoo-san*
gakuchoo	president of a university	*Gakuchoo(-sensei)*
koochoo	principal of a school	*Koochoo-sensei*

[6] This list is not exhaustive.

the head nurse, when she should have addressed her as *fuchoo-san*. The head nurse retorted, "How rude to address me as *anata*!" and walked away, refusing to comply with the last request made by the wife before the patient passed away. (Cited in *Keigo no shinsetsu na tsukaikata*, by T. Tsujimura.) This is another true-life example of how insulting the word *anata* can be to the Japanese.

Heads of a lower division within a company, agency, or institution, such as *buchoo* (division head), *kachoo* (department head), *kakarichoo* (section head, supervisor), and *gakubuchoo* (dean) are addressed by their titles by colleagues and subordinates, but not necessarily by people outside their workplace. In other words, only those who are public figures, in the sense that their professions or positions put them in contact with the public, are addressed by their titles by everybody. In most work settings, one addresses and refers to heads of sections, divisions, and so on, by the title alone without *-san*, but there are places where one does attach *-san* after the title, such as *buchoo-san*. How one should address one's boss, therefore, depends on the customary address form used in that particular workplace.

It should be added here that the title is generally not used as an address term by individuals who are direct superiors of those with titles. Their superiors will address them as LN-*san*.

Other Titles. There are many other titles for people in high positions that do not end in *-choo*, such as *chiji* (governor), *daijin* (minister), *taishi* (ambassador), and *sooryooji* (consul general). In addressing these individuals, one does NOT attach *-san* to the title. One addresses them by the title alone, or LN + title.

NAME WITH HONORIFIC SUFFIX

People without titles, or people one associates with in a context where the title is not used, are addressed with an honorific suffix. The exceptions to this general rule may be found among address terms used by some members within the family, by an increasing number of today's youth, and in journalistic reporting. The various honorific suffixes are as follows.

-san

The most common way to address an adult who does not fall into any of the title categories above is the last name (LN) plus *-san*, regardless of sex, age, marital status, or social status. The honorific suffix *-san* can be attached to the last name, first name, occupation, name of store, kinship term, etc. to address a person or to refer to the person. It is the most widely used of the group of honorific suffixes *-sama*, *-san*, *-kun*, *-chan*, and *-chama*.

LN + *-san*. Interestingly, despite the lack of sexual equality and the existence of male and female speech in Japan, no distinction is made in addressing a man and a woman, married or single. All are addressed in the same way with *-san*. Thus it is impossible to discern the gender of the person when one hears out of context just the last name plus *-san*.

You will recall that the *-choo* title for positions at the intermediate level of hierarchy in a workplace is used as an address term only by colleagues and subordinates. Thus, in situations where the addressee has such a position title in his company, but you are neither an employee of the same company nor have any business dealings with his company, and are speaking to him just as a personal acquaintance, the way to address him is with LN + *-san*, like *Tanaka-san*.

Name of company + *-san*. The name of a company with *-san* is also used in place of a second person pronoun ("your" company) or to refer to another company in the third person in business talks, such as *Sanseidoo-san* or *Mitsubishi Shooji-san*.

Occupation + *-san*. The honorific suffix *-san* can also be used with the name of an occupation in addressing or referring to a person in that occupation, particularly when the last name of the person is not known to the speaker. A policeman (*junsa*) is addressed and referred to as *omawari-san*, a mail delivery man as *yuubinya-san*, a carpenter as *daiku-san*, a driver or chauffeur as *untenshu-san*, a nurse as *kangofu-san* and so on. All types of stores ending with *-ya*, such as *hon-ya* (book store), *kusuri-ya* (drug store), *sushi-ya* (sushi restaurant), are often referred to as _____*ya-san*. The owner of the store, as well as a delivery boy from that store, can also be addressed in this manner.

Service personnel such as salesclerks and employees of banks, stores, restaurants, and hotels address their customers *okyaku-san*

(Mr./Ms. Guest/Customer), and whoever accompanies the customer as *otsure-san*. The customer is always treated with respect as a higher-status person. The customer, on the other hand, may use *anata* in return and speak at the N level to the service person, although many women choose to speak at the P-0 level.

Kinship Terms + -*san*. In addressing family members older than the speaker, and in referring to family members of the addressee and others, -*san* is attached to the kinship term. Because of the complexity, details are given in the section on "Kinship Terms" later in this chapter.

Last Name vs. First Name. Since -*san* can be attached to either LN or FN, a discussion on the difference between the use of LN and FN is in order. Children use FN with an honorific suffix (-*chan*, -*kun*), among themselves, and from the time they are in high school, they begin to use LN-*san* with their friends. Today, however, in imitation of the West, the use of FN is extending to the college age, and often without any honorific suffix. Among adults, FN plus an honorific suffix (-*san*, -*kun*, -*chan*) is used to address someone whom one has known since the childhood of the addressee, or when one knows the whole family and is addressing a younger member of that family. The use of FN usually goes with N-level speech.

-*sama*

The most respectful of the group of honorific suffixes, -*sama*, has limited usage. It is used with kinship terms in addressing or referring to a family member of the addressee when one wants to be very polite, such as "*Otoo-sama (wa) ikaga de irasshaimasu ka?*" (How is your father?) Otherwise, -*sama* is usually not attached to a last name or first name except in addressing letters.

-*kun*

Men often use -*kun* instead of -*san* at the N level of speech, that is to say, in addressing or referring to intimate equals and lower-status people, except family members. Sons or younger brothers are never addressed with -*kun*. It is not exactly equivalent to -*san*, since -*kun* can be used only in N-level speech, while -*san* can be used in P-level speech in addressing even a higher-status person. Unlike the broadly applicable -*san*, -*kun* can be attached only to FN and LN, and not to kinship terms, store names, or occupations. Traditionally -*kun* was used by male speakers, sometimes even in addressing a lower-status woman, such as a male high school teacher addressing all his students, male and female, with LN-*kun*. In recent years the determinant for the gender-specific -*kun* has shifted from the gender of the speaker to that of the addressee. Girls from kindergarten up address their male classmates FN-*kun* and female classmates FN-*san* or FN-*chan*. The use of -*kun* by women generally stops when they leave the school environment, except in addressing former male classmates whom they were already addressing with -*kun* in their school days. Among adult males, if the speaker has known the addressee from the time the addressee was young, he may address him as FN-*kun*, otherwise as LN-*kun*.

-*chan*, -*chama*

One addresses children by their first name or nickname followed by the affectionate diminutive honorific -*chan* instead of -*san*. The suffix -*chan* is also used by children in addressing their elder family members, such as (*o*)*too-chan*, (*o*)*nii-chan*, *obaa-chan*. The use of -*chan* is therefore confined to addressing individuals whom the speaker was close to during his own childhood, or to addressing small children. For this reason, -*chan* is never attached to the last name of a person. Today, however, younger women tend to use FN-*chan* to friends they have come to know after reaching adulthood. In some better families, -*chama*, the affectionate, diminutive version of *sama*, is used in addressing the elders in the family by the children. The parents then would refer to these adult members of the family the same way the children address them, like *obaa-chan* or *obaa-chama*, whatever the case may be. (See "Speaking to Children" below.)

How to Say "You"

Address Term as "YOU"

It has already been pointed out in Rule 2 that one generally uses the address term in place of the word "you." This rule is not restricted to P-level speech, where it is a must because the second person pronoun *anata* is taboo. At the N level also, where second person pronouns are available, one often applies this rule.

Even at the N level, one must apply this rule in speaking to family members who are older than you. In speaking to small children outside the family too, one generally uses the address term in place of a second person pronoun. With intimate friends equal or lower in status, and with younger members of the family (one's son, daughter, younger brother, or younger sister), one has the choice of either using a second person pronoun or the address term. In other words, one can safely manage without using the second person pronoun "you" altogether. A few examples are given below.

(1) "FN / Mr. / Ms._____, is this **yours**?"
   N: M: *Kiyoshi-kun, kore Kiyoshi-kun no kai?*
       F: *Kiyoshi-chan, kore Kiyoshi-chan no?*
   P-0: *Tanaka-san, kore (wa) Tanaka-san no desu ka?*
   P-1: *Watanabe Sensei, kore (wa) (Watanabe) sensei no deshoo ka?*
   P-2: *Inchoo Sensei, kore wa Inchoo Sensei no de gozaimasuka?*

(2) "When **you** went yesterday, was it crowded?"
   N: M: *Tanaka-kun ga kinoo itta toki, kondeta ka(i)?*
       F: *Tanaka-san ga kinoo itta toki, kondeta (no)?*
   P-0: *Tanaka-san ga kinoo itta toki, konde(i)mashita ka?*
   P-1: *(Tanaka-san ga) kinoo irasshatta toki, konde imashita ka?*
   P-2: *(Kachoo ga) kinoo o-ide ni natta toki wa konde imashita deshoo ka?*

At all levels in (1), the first word is an address term, while the repetition of it in the sentence serves as a second person reference term, meaning "you." In (2), there is no address term, only the use of the address term in place of the second person pronoun.

Anata

Anata **is an N-level second person pronoun that is used in addressing someone definitely younger or lower in status, or an intimate equal.** It is used more frequently by women, because men have another pronoun, *kimi*, available to them. The contracted form ***anta*** is used by women in more informal speech within the N level.

In male speech, which tends to be less polite than female speech, *anata* is sometimes used at the P-0 level, not only to complete strangers, but also to address a non-intimate person at the equal level or to a lower-status person in a formal, distant way, but certainly never to a higher-status person. In informal N-level speech, men use the pronoun ***kimi*** to address both men and women, although some men use *anata* for women.

The N-level sentences in (1), given above, could also be said with the second person pronoun as follows:

(3) "FN (in the U.S.), is this yours?"
    N: M: *Haruo-kun (FN), kore kimi no kai?*
           Tanaka-kun (LN), kore kimi no kai?
      F: *Haruo-san, kore anata no?*
        Tanaka-san, kore anata no?

As has been repeatedly emphasized, *anata* is not to be used in P-level speech. One exception is in addressing a complete stranger (*aka no tanin*) at the P-0 level, as in the following example.

(4) "Mr./Ms., you dropped something."
    P-0: *Moshimoshi, anata nani ka otoshimashita yo.*
    P-1: ***Moshimoshi, nani ka otosaremashita yo.*** /
         Moshimoshi, nani ka o-otoshi ni narimashita yo.

At the P-0 level of minimum politeness, no special respect is shown to the addressee, except to maintain a formal distance. At the slightly higher P-1 level, where the use of *anata* is taboo, *oto-saremashita* and *o-otoshi ni narimashita*, the exalting forms of the verb *otosu,* make it unnecessary to use the word "you."

Kimi

At the N level, men use the term *kimi* to refer to those whom they address as *-kun*, regardless of whether LN or FN is used with *-kun*, as we saw illustrated in (3). It is a male equivalent of *anata*, to be used only to intimate equals or those younger or lower in status. *Kimi*, however, is not used in speaking to younger members of the family, just as *-kun* is not used in addressing them. *Omae* would be used instead. In the case of today's younger women, even though they learn to address their male classmates as FN/LN-*kun*, they do not use *kimi* in speaking to them, but use *anata*. Some examples are given below.

(5) "Kazuo (FN), aren't you going? I'm going, you know."
    N: M: *Kazuo-**kun**, **kimi** ikanai no ka? Ore wa iku yo.*
       F: *Kazuo-**kun**, **anata** ikanai no? Watashi wa iku wa yo.*

(6) "Mr. Tanaka, everybody is already gathered here. Where in the world have you been?"
    N: M: *Tanaka-**kun**, minna moo koko ni atsumatteru noni,*
          ***kimi** wa ittai doko ni itteta n da?*
       F: *Tanaka-**san**, minna moo koko ni atsumatteru noni,*
          ***anata** wa ittai doko ni itteta no?*

Example (6) could be said by a higher-status person to his or her subordinate in a hierachical relationship, or by an equal intimate.

Otaku

Otaku is one term that is used at the P levels in the sense of "your house" or "your family." It is therefore not a true equivalent of "you," and is generally used in reference to personal matters. Like *uchi* ("my/our house or family"), *otaku* often connotes plurality. Just as one can say *uchi no kaisha* to refer to the company one works for, one can refer to the addressee's company as *otaku no kaisha*. Some examples of its usage are given below.

(7) "Isn't it wonderful that your garden is so big! (that at your house the garden is so spacious)"
   P-1: *Otaku wa niwa ga hirokute, kekkoo desu nee.*
   P-2: *Otaku wa oniwa ga hirokute, kekkoo de gozaimasu nee.*

(8) "Which school has your family decided on for your son?"
   P-1: *Otaku dewa botchan no gakkoo doko ni nasaimashita ka?*
   P-2: *Otaku dewa botchan no gakkoo o dochira ni okime ni narimashita ka?*

(9) "I understand that your daughter is going to study in America."
   P-1: *Otaku no ojoosan (wa) Amerika ni ryuugaku sareru soo desu ne.*
   P-2: *Otaku no ojoosan wa Amerika ni ryuugaku nasaru to ka o-ukagai itashimashita ga . . .*

(10) "Was it in Chicago or New York that your company has its American branch office?"
   P-1: *Otaku no Amerika shiten wa Shikago deshita ka, Nyu-uyooku deshita ka?*

As can be seen, *otaku* is more frequently used in reference to the addressee's family and home, and thus tends to be used more by women. To a person normally addressed by a title, one would say "title + *no* + *otaku*," such as *sensei no otaku*, in place of just *otaku* in the above examples. In (9), we see another device used to make the statement more polite—leaving the sentence incomplete.

How to Say "I"

The standard first person pronoun introduced in language texts is *watakushi*. *Watakushi*, however, is a rather formal word, and tends to be used on more formal occasions at the P-2 level, when one carefully articulates every word one utters. At the P-1 level of politeness *watashi* is usually sufficient for both men and women. At the N level, men use *boku* or *ore*, *ore* being more informal than *boku*, while for women the more informal version of "I" is the further contracted form *atashi*, used in conjunction with *anta* for *anata*.

In using the word "I" minimally, the possessive pronoun "my" must also be omitted whenever possible. Since Japanese nouns do not require an article or a possessive pronoun to precede them, in a sentence like "I forgot to bring my dictionary," the "my" is extraneous in the equivalent Japanese sentence. The group-oriented Japanese also use *uchi* to mean "we," and *uchi no* for "our," in place of "my" in phrases like "my company," "my department," and even "my father" (in contrast to "yours").

Self-reference terms at the P levels are not as complex as address terms. Only at the N level in relation to children does the use of the self-reference term deviate because adults do not use the word "I" (*boku*, *watashi*, etc.) when they speak to children. (See the section "Speaking to Children" in this chapter.)

Let us look at some sample sentences where "you" and "I" are involved.

(11) "Have you seen the site of this morning's fire? I went to see it during lunchtime. It's horrible."

> N:M: *Kimi kesa no kaji no ato mita kai? Boku hiruyasumi ni mite kita n da ga, monosugoi zo.*

> P-0: *Anata wa kesa no kaji no ato mimashita ka? Boku hiruyasumi ni mite kimashita ga, monosugoi desu yo.*

> P-1: **Ka-choo/Tanaka-san (wa) kesa no kaji no ato (o) go-ran ni narimashita ka? Watashi wa hiruyasumi ni mite kimashita ga, monosugoi desu yo.**

N: F: *Anata kesa no kaji no ato mita? Watashi/Atashi hiruyasumi ni mite kita kedo, monosugoi wa yo.*

F+: *Akiko-san kesa no kaji no ato goran ni natta? Watashi o-hiruyasumi ni mite kita kedo, monosugoi wa yo.*

P-0: *Tanaka-san kesa no kaji no ato mimashita ka? Watashi o-hiruyasumi ni mite kimashita ga, monosugoi desu yo.*

P-1: **Tanaka-san wa kesa no kaji no ato o goran ni narimashita ka? Watashi wa o-hiruyasumi ni mite mairimashita ga, monosugoi desu.**

P-2: *Ka-choo/Tanaka-san wa kesa no kaji no ato goran ni narimashita deshoo ka? Watakushi wa o-hiruyasumi ni mite mairimashita ga, monosugoo gozaimashita.*

Note that women use *watashi* at a lower level of speech than men do, namely from the N level, while men use it only from the P-1 level. The use of *anata* at the P-0 level by men means that the addressee is either a distant equal or a lower-status person whom the speaker addresses politely. Women generally do not use *anata* in P-level speech.

Reference to a Third Person: In-Group and Out-Group Members

Reference to a third person requires determining first whether or not the third person is a member of the speaker's in-group or the addressee's group. Members of the speaker's own group are treated in the same way as the speaker treats himself, namely with humbling terms, while members of the addressee's group are treated with exalting terms. This is particularly important in reference to family members, which will be discussed under "Kinship Terms."

There are no commonly used third person pronouns in Japanese. Once the name of the person is mentioned, there is no reason to repeat reference to that person, as in the case of "you" and "I," except for emphasis, contrast, or clarification. The terms **kare** (he) and **kanojo** (she) are used by the postwar generation generally with the meaning "boyfriend" and "girlfriend." The phrases *ano hito* or *ano kata* serve as the third person pronoun, without regard to gender, both meaning "that person" with the latter showing respect for the third person.

WORK SETTINGS

The in-group/out-group distinction becomes relevant in work situations, when one speaks for or represents the company or agency one works for. To treat members of one's own group with humbling terms in such a situation means also dispensing with titles or -*san* when referring to in-group members no matter how high in rank.

To an out-group person, such as a caller from outside or a visitor, the secretary would refer to her boss in humbling terms, while to another employee of the company, an in-group member, she would use exalting terms to refer to the same boss.

(12) "Mr. Suzuki is in conference now and is not here." (P-1)

> To an out-group member: *Suzuki wa ima kaigichuu de orimasen.*

> To an in-group member: *Suzuki-kachoo wa ima kaigichuu de irasshaimasen.*
>
> *Suzuki-kachoo wa ima kaigichuu de oide ni narimasen.*

As can be seen, within the company, the hierarchy is strictly observed, and the secretary would address her boss and refer to him when speaking to another in-group member with the appropriate title and verbs of exaltation. This is in great contrast to the American way, where the secretary may address her boss by his first name "Bob," but would refer to him as "Mr. Smith" to an outsider.

The in-group/out-group distinction, however, is a relative one. Once I called my brother at his office and said to his secretary, *Niyekawa no ane desu ga, otooto wa orimasu deshoo ka* ("This is Niyekawa's elder sister, but is my brother there?"). She responded, probably by habit, *Niyekawa wa ima kaigichuu de seki o hazushite orimasu* ("Niyekawa is in conference now and not at his seat") in humbling terms. In this situation, her boss was a family member of the addressee, so the in-group/out-group frame had temporarily changed. She was supposed to treat her boss as a member of the addressee's group, and refer to him in the same exalting way as the addressee herself. She should have said, *Niyekawa-buchoo wa ima kaigichuu de o-seki o hazushite oide desu* or *hazushite irasshaimasu.*

NON-WORK SETTINGS

When one is not representing one's company, however, the in-group/out-group distinction in terms of one's workplace recedes into the background, and one need not be concerned with it. There is no need to use humble terms in speaking about one's boss, nor exalting terms for the addressee's boss. They are treated just as third persons. Generally the only relevant in-group/out-group concern in non-business conversation is family members of the speaker and the addressee.

NEUTRAL THIRD PERSON

If the third person does not belong to either the speaker's group or the addressee's group, is in no way related to the addressee, and is not present as a listener in the conversation, then it is a matter of your personal speech style or your feeling towards the third person that determines how you should refer to him and his actions. If he is of higher status, or you have respect for him, or feel the addressee has respect for him, or if it is your style to speak politely, you can refer to him with exalting expressions; if not, you may use neutral expressions.

(13) "Mr. Yamada didn't come yesterday."
　　　P-0: *Yamada-san wa kinoo kimasen deshita.*
　　　P-1: *Yamada-san wa kinoo koraremasen deshita.*
　　　P-2: *Yamada-san wa sakujitsu oide ni narimasen deshita.*
　　　　　 Yamada-san wa sakujitsu konakatta n(o) de gozaimasu yo.
　　　　　 (You know, Mr./Ms Yamada didn't come.)

As can be seen, at the P-2 level, one would use the exalting form for a third person, unless he or she is of lower status than both the speaker and the addressee, or the speaker has contempt for him, as expressed in the last sentence, where the additional connotation "I'm telling you" is present. If an exalted form is to be used for *Yamada-san*, *konakatta* should be replaced by *irassharanakatta* or *oide ni naranakatta* (in the nonpolite style, since the phrase modifies the noun *no/n*). Among the younger people today, however, the tendency is not to apply exalted forms for a third person who is not a listener to the conversation, and use respect forms only in relation to the addressee and members of the addressee's group.

Kinship Terms: In-Group and Out-Group

A brief reference to kinship terms was made in Chapter 2. There are essentially two sets of terms: one set that is neutral, used as humble words to refer to one's own family members, and another that is exalting, to be used to refer to family members of the addressee and other out-group members. The exalting terms are also used when addressing elder members of one's own family. A list of these is provided in Chart 11.

IN INTERACTION WITH OUT-GROUP PERSONS

The exalting terms in the rightmost column of the chart are used to refer to kin of the addressee as well as of any other outgroup person, such as *otoo-san* for "your" or "his" father. The nonasterisked terms are also used as address terms to such members. Exalting terms should not be used to refer to one's own kin. This applies even to N-level speech.

Making Reference to Family Members of the Addressee

(14) "With your husband away from home, it must be difficult for you."

Chart 11: Kinship Address and Reference Terms

Relationship	Own Family Reference Term ("my")	Address Term	Others Reference Term ("your," "his," "her")[8]
grandfather	*sofu*	*o-jii-san*	*o-jii-san*
grandmother	*sobo*	*o-baa-san*	*o-baa-san*
grandparents	*sofubo*	—	—
father	*chichi*	*o-too-san*	*o-too-san*
mother	*haha*	*o-kaa-san*	*o-kaa-san*
parent	*oya*	—	—
parents	*ryooshin*	—	*go-ryooshin*[8]
brother, elder	*ani*	*o-nii-san*	*o-nii-san*
younger	*otooto*	FN (*-san*)	*otooto-san*[8]
sister, elder	*ane*	*o-nee-san*	*o-nee-san*
younger	*imooto*	FN (*-san*)	*imooto-san*[8]
siblings	*kyoodai*	—	*go-kyoodai*[8]
husband	*shujin*[7] /LN	*anata* FN-*san*	*go-shujin* (*-san*)[8]
wife	*kanai*[7]	FN	*oku-san*
son	*musuko*	FN (*-san*)	*musuko-san*[8]/ *botchan*
daughter	*musume*	FN (*-san*)	*o-joo-san*
child/children	*kodomo*	—	*o-ko-san*[8]
family	*kazoku*	—	*go-kazoku*[8]
uncle	*oji*	*oji-san*	*oji-san*
aunt	*oba*	*oba-san*	*oba-san*
nephew	*oi*	FN-*san*	*oigo-san*[8]
niece	*mei*	FN-*san*	*meigo-san*[8]
cousin	*itoko*	FN-*san*	*itoko-san*[8]

Relationship	Own Family Reference Term ("my")	Address Term	Others Reference Term ("your," "his," "her")[8]
IN-LAWS			
father-in-law	*shuuto*	*o-too-san*	*o-shuuto-san*[8]
mother-in-law	*shuutome*	*o-kaa-san*	*o-shuutome-san*[8]
son-in-law	*muko*	FN-*san*	*o-muko-san*[8]
daughter-in-law	*yome*	FN-*san*	*o-yome-san*[8]
brother-in-law			
a) elder	*giri no ani*	*o-nii-san*	*giri no o-nii-san*[8]
b) younger	*giri no otooto*	FN-*san*	*giri no otooto-san*[8]
sister-in law			
a) elder	*giri no ane*	*o-nee-san*	*giri no o-nee-san*[8]
b) younger	*giri no imooto*	FN-*san*	*giri no imooto-san*[8]
brothers- & sisters-in law	*kojuuto*		*kojuuto-san*[8]

The honorific suffix -san in all cases can be replaced by -sama, chan, or -chama. "Elder" and "younger" are not determined by absolute age, but by the theoretical hierarchy of the family. (See diagram 3 on p. 103.)

[7] Reference term for one's own family members given in the second column are also neutral dictionary terms except those marked with [7]. The neutral dictionary term for "husband" is *otto*, "wife" *tsuma*.

[8] Reference terms for family members of others can also be used as address terms to them except those marked with[8].

N: M: *Goshujin (ga) rusu de, anta/kimi mo taihen da na.*
  F: *Goshujin (ga) rusu de, anata mo taihen ne.*
  P-0: *Goshujin ga rusu de, LN-san mo taihen desu ne.*
  **P-1: Goshujin ga orusu de, LN-san mo taihen de
    irasshaimasu ne.**
  P-2: *Goshujin-sama ga orusu de, LN-san mo taihen de
    irasshaimasu ne.*

(15) "Is your father back from Hokkaidoo?"
  N: M: *Otoo-san moo Hokkaidoo kara kaette kita kai?*
    F: *Otoo-san moo Hokkaidoo kara kaette kita no?*
    F +: *Otoo-san moo Hokkaidoo kara okaeri ni natta no?*
    **P-1: Otoo-sama wa moo Hokkaidoo kara okaeri ni nari
      mashita ka?**
    P-2: *Otoo-sama wa moo Hokkaidoo kara okaeri ni natta
      no de gozaimasu ka?*

(16) "I hear your younger sister is getting married."
  N: M/F: *Imooto-san kekkon suru n datte ne.*
    P-0: *Imooto-san kekkon suru n desutte ne.*
    P-1: Imooto-san kekkon nasaru n da soo desu ne.
    P-2: *Imooto-san ga gokekkon nasaru no da soo de
      gozaimasu ne.*

As can be seen, the level of speech makes little difference in the
term used to refer to the addressee's family member. The only
change is the shift from *-san* to *-sama* at higher levels of formality
when the person referred to is an elder or higher-status person in
the addressee's family.

Addressing Members of Friend's Family

If the norm is to address your speaking partner as LN-*san*, how
do you address his or her family members when you are invited to
their home where all the family members go by the same last
name? In situations like this, you adopt the perspective of your
friend, who is the link in your relationship to his family members.

You address each of his family members more or less the way your friend addresses them, ignoring the age differences between you yourself and the person. If he calls his parents *Papa* and *Mama*, you address them also *Papa* and *Mama*. However, if he calls his parents *Otoo-chan* and *Okaa-chan*, it is more appropriate to use the more polite form *Otoo-san*, *Okaa-san*. The person your friend addresses *Onii-san* (elder brother) or *Onee-san* (elder sister) will be addressed *Onii-san* or *Onee-san* by you also. Similarly younger siblings or children are addressed in the same way your friend addresses them, except that you should attach *-san* or *-chan* to the first name even if he does not. The effect of taking the point of view of the person serving as a link can make the address term sound strange at times. For instance, I am addressed *Onee-san* by my brother's mother-in-law. Her relationship to me is through her daughter, who is married to my younger brother. Since her daughter, her "link" to me, calls me *Onee-san*, she also addresses me *Onee-san*, even though she is one generation older than I am.

The rule of substituting the address term for the word "you" in speaking to a person of higher status applies here too. To a person younger than yourself, you can use *anata*. If you are a male and are speaking to your friend's younger brother, and if he is definitely younger than you yourself, you can use *kimi* to him. It is also perfectly acceptable to use the address term in place of "you" to younger people. Examples follow.

(17) "Do you play golf?" Said to your friend's:
   Father: *Otoo-sama/-san wa gorufu nasaimasu ka?*
   Elder sister: *Onee-san wa gorufu nasaimasu ka?*
   Younger brother, adult: *FN-san/-kun wa gorufu shimasu ka?*

(18) "May I have a look at your watch?" Said to your friend's:
   Grandfather: *Ojii-sama/-san no tokei chotto haiken sasete itadakemasu ka?*
   Mother: *Okaa-sama/-san no tokei chotto haiken sasete itadakemasu ka?*

Younger sister, adult: *FN-san no tokei chotto misete itadake masu/moraemasu ka?*
Younger sister, child: *FN-chan no tokei chotto misete kureru?*

In (17), all addressees are adults, hence the questions are in P-level speech. Men might say to the younger brother, if he is also much younger than the speaker, *FN-kun wa gorufu suru ka?* In (18), a donatory verb (see Chapter 6) has to be used. Whenever there is the slash mark /, the first version shows the greater respect, and tends to be used by women, while the second less polite version tends to be used by men. The question addressed to the child is in N, and has a slightly different meaning. It is more direct and says "Will you show me your watch?" while the others have the literal meaning of "Would you be willing to do me the favor of showing me your watch?"

Students. If you and your friend are students, once you meet your friend's family, you may address your friend from this point on by the first name plus *-san* or *-kun*.

Spouses. If your friend is a married man, you can continue to address him the way you have been. You address his wife as *Okusan*. If, on the other hand, your link to the family members is through a married woman whom you have been addressing by her last name plus *-san*, then you will have to use that address term for her husband, and call her by the first name plus *-san*. However, in situations of this sort, the Japanese generally try to avoid using address terms to either of them. The younger generation would show less hesitancy in addressing both of them by their first name plus *-san*. If the woman is a professional who goes by a different last name, then each can be addressed by their respective last names plus *-san* without any problem.

Referring to One's Own Family Members: Humble Kinship Terms
When one refers to one's own family (in-group) members in

speaking or writing to a non-family (out-group) member, the set of humble kinship terms in the second column of Chart 11 is used, even at the N level of speech. These kinship terms, with the exception of *shujin* (my husband) and *kanai* (my wife), are the kinship terms listed in the dictionary, and are used as neutral words in objective journalistic writing. Children above the age of ten are expected to start using such humbling terms in referring to their own family members. In other words, when a neutral kinship term, such as *haha*, is used in conversation or in letters, it can only mean "my" mother, and therefore makes the possessive "my" unnecessary.

(19) "I can't go because my father is sick."
    N: M: *Chichi/Oyaji ga byooki da kara, (boku) ikarenai n da.*
       F: *Chichi ga byooki da kara, (watashi) ikarenai no.*
    P-0: *Chichi ga byooki desu kara, (boku/watashi wa) ikare nai n desu.*
    P-1: ***Chichi ga byooki desu kara, watashi wa mairemasen ga . . .***
    P-2: *Chichi ga byooki de gozaimasu kara, watakushi wa zannen nagara ikarenai n(o) de gozaimasu.*

In the above set, with the exception of P-1, every sentence contains *no/n*, which provides the explanatory meaning of "It is because my father is sick that I can't go." The reason why P-1 is different is that the humble verb *mairimasu* is seldom used in the plain form *mairu*. It would be odd to say *Watashi wa mairenai n desu*. It is equally odd to say *Watashi wa mairemasen no desu*. The word *oyaji* ("my old man") in N: M is often used by men in place of *chichi* among intimates. The counterpart for *haha* ("mother") is *ofukuro*. The P-2 sentence contains *zannen nagara* ("regrettably") to make the statement more humble.

Younger Members. Generally among non-intimates, that is when P-level speech is used, one refers to one's own family member by the humble kinship term. However, between acquaintances, such as neighbors, who know each other's family members by name, one may refer to one's younger member of the family, such as one's son, or younger sister, by the first name. In such cases, the honorific suffix -*san* is never attached. In N-level speech, however, it is all right to refer to that member by the way one addresses him, such as *Aki-chan* or *uchi no Aki-chan*. If kinship terms are used, only humble ones are used even at the N level.

Spouses. Though *shujin* and *kanai* are the most common reference terms, note that women often refer to their husband by LN only, just as the secretary refers to her boss by LN without -*san* or title to visitors or callers from outside. A woman whose husband changed his LN to hers through marriage naturally cannot do so. There are also *uchi no hito* and *taku* (my house) as substitutes for the term *shujin*.

IN-GROUP INTERACTION WITHIN ONE'S OWN FAMILY

How one addresses members of one's own family depends on the hierarchical relationship between the speaker and the addressee. Just as in a work setting, it is within the in-group that the hierarchy is most strictly observed. While non-Japanese need not worry how to address their own family members, a working knowledge of kinship terms is necessary for communication, and for those marrying into a Japanese family, it is essential. As Column 3 in Chart 11 indicates, individuals who rank higher and lower than the speaker in the family are addressed differently.

Addressing Elders in Own Family

Exalting kinship terms are used to address elder members of one's own family. "Elder" here means not only in absolute age, but also in terms of the theoretical hierarchy. The wife of your uncle or of your elder brother may be younger than you in absolute age, but as the wife of your uncle, who is one generation ahead of you, or of your elder brother, she must be treated as an elder, your *meue*, and be addressed as *Oba-san* (aunt) or *Onee-san* (elder sister), and not by FN-*san* until she asks you to call her so. As is the case outside the family, instead of *anata*, the address term is used in place of "you" when speaking with elders in the family.

While the standard kinship address term takes -*san*, as was mentioned before, -*chan* is also used. Grandparents, in particular, tend to be addressed with -*chan*, and in some families with -*chama*, the diminutive version of -*sama*. In urban middle-class families, children are taught to address their parents *papa* and *mama* until their teens.

Some examples of saying "you" to a family member are given below.

(20) "When are you going to Hokkaido?" (to an uncle)
    N: M/F: *Oji-san (wa) itsu Hokkaidoo ni iku no?*
    P-1: *Oji-san wa itsu Hokkaidoo ni irassharu n desu ka?*

(21) "Let me see your new camera" (to Father)
    N: M/F: *Papa/Otoo-san/Otoo-chan no atarashii kamera misete.*
    P-1: *Otoo-san no atarashii kamera misete kudasai.*

P or N? While in most families, all members use N-level speech to one another, the daughter-in-law and son-in-law speak at the P-1 level to their elder in-laws (see "Speaking to In-Laws" below). In some upper-class traditional families, children speak in P to their parents, grandparents, and other adult relatives. In such families, it is not uncommon to find children addressing their grandparents with -*chama* instead of -*chan*, like *obaa-chama*.

The address term used in addressing elder members of the family is not only used in place of the second person pronoun "you," but also in referring to that person when speaking with other members of the family, as follows:

(22) "I can't go out until Dad comes home, can I?"
    N: M: *Otoo-san/Otoo-chan/Papa ga kaette kuru made, ore dekakerarenai na.*

F: *Otoo-san/Otoo-chan/Papa ga kaette kuru made,*
    watashi dekakerarenai wa ne.

This can be said to any member of the family, including the father.

Speaking to In-Laws

The question of whether in-laws are in-group members or not may come to mind. As was pointed out earlier, the in-group/out-group distinction is a relative one. When one is speaking to a non-family member, in-laws are in-group members and must be referred to in humble terms, such as *giri no ane*, or *shujin no otooto*, with corresponding humbling verbs. When a wife speaks to her in-laws, elder in age or theoretical hierarchy, she must use P-1. Suppose she is speaking to her husband's parents. Her husband is an in-group member, but he is also the son of the addressee, thus an out-group member in this situation. Should she use humbling verbs about her husband's actions or exalting verbs? Let us examine the three possible expressions given below.

(23) "Just at that time my husband came home."
    a) *Choodo sono toki **shujin** ga kaette **mairi**mashita.*
    b) *Choodo sono toki **FN-san** ga kaette **irasshai**mashita.*
    c) *Choodo sono toki **FN-san** ga kaette kimashita.*

Sentence a) treats the husband as an in-group member with a humbling verb, b) treats him as an out-group member with an exalting verb, and c) treats him neutrally. People, including grammarians, vary in their opinions as to which version should be used in this situation. Parents, particularly mothers, often feel that the daughter-in-law has taken away their son. To use the a) version means to consider him as a member of "my" group and NOT "yours," reinforcing the mother's feeling. My recommendation is to avoid a) and to use the neutral c), probably the least controversial.

It might be added here that the substitutes for *shujin* listed previously (LN, *uchi no hito*, *taku*) are not acceptable in speaking to one's in-laws.

Addressing a Younger Member of One's Own Family

Younger members of one's own family are addressed by their first name plus either -*san* or -*chan*, but not -*kun*. Children, particularly boys, may be addressed by their first name only without -*san* or -*chan* by their parents, grandparents, and elder siblings. To say "you," besides *anata*, the familiar **omae** is available within the immediate family only. *Kimi*, however, is not used within the family, just as -*kun* is not. As was pointed out earlier, the address term is frequently substituted for the word "you."

Adults in speaking to children do not use the word "I" to refer to themselves, as shown below.

Speaking to Children

In addressing children of elementary school age and below, their first name or nickname is followed by the diminutive honorific -*chan* instead of -*san*.

Adults in speaking to children use N-level speech, and do not use the first person pronoun. In referring to themselves, instead of the word "I," they use the exact term by which they are addressed by the particular child. Thus parents, grandparents, aunts, and uncles, as well as elder siblings, use *otoo-san*, *obaa-chan*, *onii-san*, or whatever the case may be, instead of *boku* or *watashi*. Kindergarten and elementary school teachers refer to themselves as *sensei* when they speak to the children. An example is given below.

(24) "I'm against it." Said by:
    Father: *Otoo-san/Otoo-chan/Papa wa hantai da ne.*
    Grandmother: *Obaa-san/Obaa-chan wa hantai yo.*
    Elementary school teacher: M: *Sensei wa hantai da ne.*
                                F: *Sensei wa hantai yo.*

An elder brother who is addressed *onii-san* by his younger siblings will say *Oniisan wa hantai da* in the above case, but in the small nuclear family in large metropolitan areas today, there is a trend to address elder siblings by their first name only or with -*chan*. In such families, the elder brother would refer to himself as *boku* or *ore*, and the elder sister as *watashi* or by the way she is addressed, such as *Haruko* or *Haru-chan wa hantai yo*.

(Some girls use their first names in place of "I" in speaking to their friends.)

Diagram 2 (from *Words in Context*, by T. Suzuki) expresses well the complexity involved in addressing individuals in various relationships, and how to say "you" and "I" in relation to each of them.

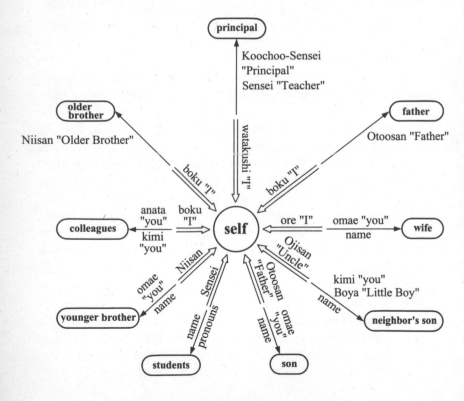

Diagram 2

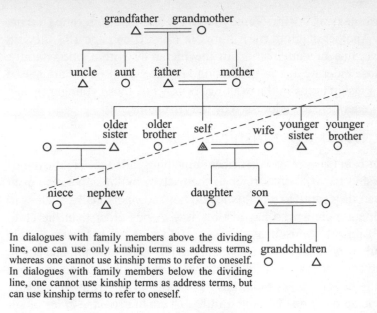

In dialogues with family members above the dividing line, one can use only kinship terms as address terms, whereas one cannot use kinship terms to refer to oneself. In dialogues with family members below the dividing line, one cannot use kinship terms as address terms, but can use kinship terms to refer to oneself.

Diagram 3

The above diagram may be summarized as follows (Chart 12):

Chart 12: Address and Self-Reference Terms within the Family

Status of Addressee	Address Term	Self-Reference Term
Higher	Honorific Kinship Term	Pronoun M: *boku, ore* F: *watashi*
Lower Adult	First Name (*-san*)	Pronoun M: *boku, ore* F: *watashi*
Child	First Name (*-chan*)	Honorific Kinship Term: the term by which he/she is addressed

Summary of Within-Family Address and Self-Reference Terms

Another diagram from *Words in Context* on page 103 shows a clear line of demarcation in the hierarchy within one's family. Those elder by age or generation and their spouses are addressed by kinship terms in the exalting form, while those younger by age or generation are addressed by the first name.

FICTIVE USE OF KINSHIP TERMS

Words in Context also describes something called the fictive use of kinship terms. Adults refer to themselves by kinship terms even when they speak to a child they do not know personally, such as in helping a child who has lost his way. A boy older than the child will refer to himself as *onii-chan* (elder or big brother), a male adult as *oji-chan* (uncle), a woman as *oba-chan* (auntie), and so on. The child, if male and five years or younger, is addressed as *booya* (little boy) or *boku*, older boys as *onii-chan*, a girl as *onee-chan*. Thus an older girl helping a little girl could use *onee-chan* in addressing the girl as well as to refer to herself, like *Onee-chan doo shita no? Sa, nakanai de. Kono ookii onee-chan ga tsuite iru kara, moo daijoobu yo.* ("What happened to you, big girl? Don't cry any more. This big sister is with you, so it's okay now.")

The fictive use of kinship terms was also exemplified in the account of journalists given at the beginning of this chapter. A stranger who seems to be a father (usually because a child is with him) is addressed *otoo-san*, a married woman *okusan* (Mrs.), and so on. Before, people did not hesitate to address an older woman *obaa-san* in a similar manner, but today, adopting the Western value of "youth" and wanting to be considered younger, even grandmothers do not like to be addressed *obaa-san* by a stranger.

Expressing Plurality

In Japanese the singular/plural distinction is not made. When it is necessary to indicate plurality of persons, one may add one of the following suffixes to the noun. Alternatively, one may express "you" in plural with the word *mina-san/sama*.

-tachi. The most widely used of the group, such as in *watashi-tachi, anata-tachi, oji-san-tachi, -tachi* is neutral in the sense that it expresses no respect for the pluralized people. It may be accompanied by neutral, exalting, or humbling verbs to convey non-respect, respect for, or humility of the pluralized people respectively. *Tanaka-san-tachi* would mean "Tanaka-san and his/her group of people." However, the use of *-tachi* at P-1 and above in reference to members of the addressee's group is generally avoided. At the P-2 level, the Chinese compound *ikkoo* (party) is used in place of *-tachi*, with the honorific prefix *go-* when appropriate.

(25) "Mr./Ms. Oda's party will come tomorrow."
  P-0: *Oda-san-tachi wa ashita kimasu.*
  P-1: a) *Oda-san-tachi wa ashita irasshaimasu.*
  P-1: b)*Oda-san-tachi wa ashita mairimasu.*
  P-2: a) *Oda-san go-ikkoo wa myoonichi o-ide de gozaimasu.*
  P-2: b) *Oda no ikkoo wa myoonichi mairimasu.*

"Oda-san's party" is treated neutrally in P-0, but contrastingly in the pairs of sentences at P-1 and P-2. Sentences a) exalt the party as an out-group, while sentences b) humble it as an in-group.

-gata. The suffix *-gata* is the exalting equivalent of *-tachi*, but has extremely restricted usage—limited to a few commonly used words, such as *anata-gata, sensei-gata, kata-gata* (persons). It normally requires the use of exalting verbs, and hence it cannot be attached to *watashi*. It is, however, possible for a higher-status person to say, *Anata-gata wa nani o shite iru n desu ka?* ("What are you all doing?") without an exalting verb at the P-0 level, in a hierarchical relationship, such as a teacher to her students.

-domo. As *-domo* is the humbling equivalent of *-tachi*, it is found only in *wata(ku)shi-domo* (we), and must be accompanied by a

humbling verb. Its use is going out of style, and today only older people and sales clerks use this term.

Mina-san/-sama. Unlike the preceding suffixes, *mina-san* is a free (independent) noun that can be used as an address term as well as a reference term. At the N level, it is *minna* without the honorific suffix.

(26) "Everybody, (please) listen!"
> N: M: *Minna, yoku kike.*
> F: *Minna, yoku kiite.*
> P-0: *Mina-san, yoku kiite kudasai.*
> **P-1: *Mina-san, yoku o-kiki ni natte kudasai.***
> P-2: *Mina-sama, yoku o-kiki kudasaru yoo o-negai (ita)shi masu.*

(27) "Is everybody in your family fine?" (standard greeting)
> N: M: *Kimi n(o) (u)chi ja minna genki kai?*
> F: *Anata n(o) toko(ro) minna genki?*
> F+: *Anata n(o) toko(ro) mina-san o-genki?*
> **P-1: *(O-taku no) Mina-san o-genki de irassahimasu ka?***
> P-2: *(O-taku no) Mina-sama niwa o-kawari gozaimasen ka?*

Summary Guide

This long chapter may be summarized by the following chart (Chart 13) on address and reference terms in relation to people outside the family. It should be used with Chart 12 for terms within the family.

Chart 13: How to Address, Say "You" and "I" to People Outside the Family

Level	Addressee	Address Term	"You"	"I"
P-1 & 2	Professional	*sensei*	*sensei*	*watakushi/ watashi*
	Individual w/ title	Title (*-san*)	same as addr. term	*watakushi/ watashi*
	Higher status and non-intimate equal	LN-*san*	LN-*san*	*watashi*
P-0	stranger	——	*anata*	*watashi/boku*
N: F	close friend	LN/FN-*san* FN-*chan*	LN/FN-*san/ anata/anta*	*watashi/ atashi*
	child	FN-*chan*	FN-*chan*	*oba-san/ onee-san/etc.*
N: M	close friend	LN/FN-*kun*	LN/FN-*kun/ kimi/anata*	*boku/ore*
	child	FN-*chan*	FN-*chan*	*oji-san/ onii-san/etc.*

6. Donatory Verbs

A s mentioned in Chapter 2, the Japanese think in terms of giving and receiving favors as part of the network of obligations of *giri* and *on*. Any action done for another person tends to be expressed by a compound verb, with the action in the *-te* form, followed by a verb of giving or receiving, such as *kaite morau* (have someone write for me), *katte ageru* (buy something for someone), *okutte kudasaru* (someone sends something to me). Of course, these verbs of giving and receiving, or donatory verbs, are also used singly to refer to the giving and receiving of objects.

There are three sets of donatory verbs. The sets are distinguished as follows:

Set 1. "I" or a member of "my" group gives something to someone:
sashiageru, o-age suru, ageru, yaru

Set 2. "I" or a member of "my" group receives something from someone:
itadaku, morau

Set 3. Someone gives something to "me" or a member of "my" group:
kudasaru, kureru

A number of complex factors are involved in choosing between these eight verbs. We will start with the simplest case: giving and receiving between the speaker and the addressee, and their respective group members. From there, we will examine more complex cases. The summary section outlines a gradual study method.

Giving and Receiving between Speaker's and Addressee's Group

The first two sets have the grammatical subject in common: "I" give or "I" receive, while the last two sets have the direction in common: "I receive from you" or "you give me." Which verb to use within each set depends on the relationship between the giver and receiver. This may best be shown by the following diagrams, based on but revised from *Japan and America: A Comparative Study in Language and Culture*, by Goldstein and Tamura.

The arrows in the diagrams indicate the direction of the action, while the angle of each arrow indicates the status relationship of the giver and receiver. Set 1 is more finely differentiated than the other two sets, but in all three sets, verbs in the bottom half of the

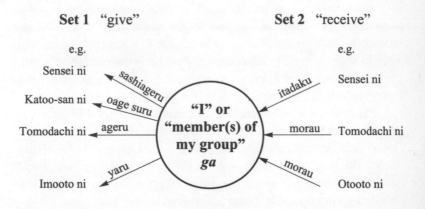

Diagram 4

Set 3 "give"

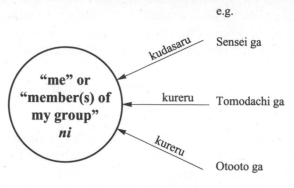

Diagram 5

diagrams—*yaru*, *morau*, and *kureru*—are generally associated with the giving to and receiving from individuals whom one would address with N when speaking directly to them, while verbs in the top part of the diagrams, namely *oage suru*, *sashiageru*, *itadaku*, and *kudasaru*, are associated with those to whom one would speak at one of the P levels. Of the two P-level verbs in Set l, *oage suru* is more often used to mention the act of giving to a third person, and not to the addressee himself.

Ageru in Set 1 is usually used in giving to someone more or less equal in status, whom you might address in N or P-0, and someone, like your father, who is higher in status but whom you would address in N. Note, however, that the verbs used in receiving from someone who is equal in status are the same as those used when referring to someone lower in status.

There is hardly any verb that is completely neutral in its meaning. Practically all of them have the connotation of either an upward or downward movement. *Ageru* comes closest to neutrality, being the only verb used solely in the horizontal direction, but if one asks a Japanese about the usage of *ageru*, many say that it is used in giving upwards, being influenced by the *kanji*   in
Thus one can say that there is no neutral word in Japanese with the meaning of "giving" or "receiving." The verbs in the top portion of

the diagrams, namely *oage suru* and *sashiageru* of Set 1, and *itadaku* of Set 2, which have "I" (or members of my group) as the grammatical subject, are humbling verbs, while *kudasaru* of Set 3, which has an out-group member or a higher-status person as the subject, is an exalting verb.

An important point to be noted about the diagrams is that "I," the speaker, is in the center and the giving/receiving action is viewed from the position of "I" in the circle. "I" can never be placed outside the circle. Hence, to say "Haruko gave me this book," one cannot say *"Haruko ga watashi ni kono hon o ageta/yatta."* To do so would mean placing "Haruko" in the circle, and "me" outside. The speaker must put himself in the circle and use a verb from Set 3 rather than Set 1, and say *Haruko ga kono hon o (watashi ni) kureta.*

EXAMPLE SENTENCES

Let us look at these verbs of giving and receiving in actual sentences. The first example of each set is about giving or receiving of objects, while the second involves the giving and receiving of a favor.

Set 1 Verbs: *sashiageru, o-age suru, ageru, yaru*
("I" or members of "my" group **give** something to someone)

(1) "Did you read the book I gave you the other day?"
  N: M: *Kono aida yatta hon wa yonda ka?*
    F: *Kono aida ageta hon wa yonda?*
  P-1: ***Kono aida sashiageta hon wa oyomi ni narimashita ka?***
  P-2: *Senjitsu sashiagemashita hon wa oyomi ni nararemashita deshoo ka?*

(2) "I'll go and buy it for you right now. (I will give you the favor of buying and coming back right away)."
  N: M: *Ima sugu katte kite yaru yo.*
    F: *Ima sugu katte kite ageru wa.*

P-1: *Ima sugu katte kite sashiagemasu.*

P-2: *Tadaima sugu ni katte kite sashiagemashoo.*

The word *yaru* has come to be perceived as crude, and women today tend to use *ageru* in its place. Some even use *ageru* in reference to animals, such as *Neko ni gohan ageta no?* ("Did you feed the cat?"). Men, however, continue to use *yaru* in "giving" to people they would address in N, such as their *meshita* (junior) and intimate equals. *Morau* and *kureru*, each being part of a set with only one other alternative, have not suffered the fate of *yaru* and continue to be used with little problem.

Set 2 Verbs: itadaku, morau
("I" or members of "my" group **receive** something from someone)

(3) "The persimmons I received from you were sweet and delicious."

    N: M: *Moratta kaki wa amakute umakatta yo.*

      F: *Itadaita/moratta kaki wa amakute oishikatta wa.*

    P-1: *Itadaita kaki wa amakute, oishikatta desu.*

    P-2: *Itadakimashita kaki wa amakute, oishuu gozaimashita.*

(4) "It was of great help to have you translate it for me." (. . . that I received from you the favor of translating)

    N: M: *Honyaku shite moratte, ooi ni tasukatta yo.*

      F: *Honyaku shite itadaite/moratte, totemo tasukatta wa.*

    P-1: *Honyaku shite itadaite, totemo tasukarimashita.*

    P-2: *Honyaku shite itadakimashite, taihen tasukarimashita.*

Set 3 Verbs: *kudasaru, kureru*
(**Someone gives** something to "**me**" or members of "my" group)

(5) "Thank you for giving my son Taroo a graduation gift."

    N: M: *Taroo ni sotsugyoo-iwai kurete, arigatoo.*

      F: *Taroo ni sotsugyoo-iwai kudasatte/kurete, arigatoo.*

    P-1: *Musuko ni sotsugyoo-iwai o kudasaimashite,*

doomo arigatoo gozaimashita.
P-2: *Musuko ni sotsugyoo-iwai o kudasaimashite, hontoo ni osore irimashita.*

(6) "Since you explained how to use it so well, I had no problem."
(Since you gave me the favor of explaining it so well, . . .)
N: M: *Tsukaikata (o) yoku setsumei shite kureta kara, mondai nakatta yo.*
F: *Tsukaikata (o) yoku setsumei shite kudasatta/kureta kara, mondai nakatta wa.*
P-1: *Tsukaikata (o) yoku setsumei shite kudasaimashita node, mondai arimasen deshita.*
P-2: *Shiyoohoo o yoku gosetsumei kudasaimashita node, mondai gozaimasen deshita.*

As can be seen, in N-level speech, directed to an intimate equal or someone lower in status, the exalting or humbling verbs need not be utilized with regard to the addressee, although donatory verbs must still be used to express favors given or received. Women, however, may reserve the lower verbs *morau* and *kureru* for only those who are clearly lower in status, and use the higher verbs *itadaku* (humbling) and *kudasaru* (exalting) when the addressee is a higher-status family member or an intimate equal.

In Sentence (5) above, we have a case where the giving from the addressee is to a family member of the speaker. There it appears perfectly natural that it is expressed as "giving downwards," because it is from an adult to a youngster. This, however, is not the reason for the "downward" motion. The true reason is the in-group/out-group principle.

As you will remember, **the in-group/out-group principle is that all in-group members are humbled, and all out-group members are exalted, regardless of age or status. In other words, across groups, hierarchy within each group is completely ignored, and people of the addressee's group are treated as if they are all of higher status, while all members of the speaker's group are treated as lower in status. As it applies to**

donatory verbs, the principle means always giving upwards to the addressee, and downwards to the speaker. Thus the speaker must, for instance, treat the addresse's child, who may be only five years old, in the same way as the addressee himself, and use *sashiageru, itadaku,* or *kudasaru* in reference to the child's action, as shown in the following examples:

(7) "Yesterday I received this from your son."
    P-1: *Kinoo (otaku no) botchan ni kore (o) itadaita n desu yo.*

Similarly, the giving by the speaker's 70-year-old mother to the addressee's child is expressed upwards rather than downwards, as follows:

(8) "I understand that my mother will read (give the favor of reading) fairy tales to your daughter again."
    P-1: *Haha ga mata ojoosan ni otogibanashi (o) yonde sashiageru soo desu.*

To an intimate equal with whom one exchanges mutual N, one may dispense with exalting and humbling terms. Women of better social background, however, may still use the humbling donatory verbs and change only the *desu* ending of the above two sentences, As intimates, they are also likely to know the first name of the child, and refer to them with *-chan* as follows:

(7) N: F+: *Kinoo Ken-chan ni kore itadaita no yo.*
(8) N: F+: *Haha ga mata Miyoko-chan ni otogibanashi yonde sashiageru soo yo.*

Others may speak to an intimate equal as if to a family member, ignoring the in-group/out-group principle, or rather treating the addressee as an in-group member, and say,

(7) N: M: *Kinoo Kenji-kun ni kore moratta yo.*
     F: *Kinoo Ken-chan ni kore moratta no yo.*

Generally, it can be said that in N-level speech, whether of intimacy or condescension (hierarchy), the speaker has the choice of either applying or ignoring the in-group/out-group principle, except the kinship terms, which are generally used even at this level. Women tend to observe the principle, while men tend to ignore it. **In P-level speech, however, it is essential that the in-group/out-group principle be observed by both parties, each treating the other as if the other is of higher status.**

Reporting of In-Group Action to Out-Group Person

We have seen that when an out-group person is the addressee, one always humbles oneself and members of one's own group. With regards to donatory verbs, this means that those verbs at the top of each set in the diagrams (*sashiageru, itadaku, kudasaru*) are reserved for reference to giving to and receiving from an out-group person. One sometimes hears a non-native speaker of Japanese say, *Kore wa otoosan ga kudasatta mono desu* ("This is something my father gave me"). Within one's own family, it is fine to use *kudasaru* for one's father, but outside the family it is not permissible to use such an exalted term for one's own father. The in-group/out-group principle must be observed, and the above person should have said, *Kore wa chichi ga kureta* (or *chichi ni moratta*) *mono desu*.

To report the giving and receiving action of family members to an out-group person, one must therefore choose the verbs at the bottom of each set, namely *yaru, morau,* and *kureru*. There is a general resistance to use *yaru*, particularly in the context of giving to one's own parents. On the other hand, even though *ageru* is used by some women in "giving" to animals, it is still considered too exalting to be used with regard to one's parents in speaking to an outsider. People find ways to get around it, as follows:

(9) "For Christmas, I gave my father a tie."
 P-1: *Kurisumasu ni wa chichi ni nekutai o kaimashita*.
  ("For Christmas I bought a tie for my father.")
  Kurisumasu ni wa chichi ni nekutai o purezento shimashita.

("For Christmas I offered a tie as a gift to my father.")

When you yourself are not involved in the action, but both giver and receiver are members of your family, then they are both "third persons," discussed below.

Both Giver and Receiver are Third Persons

We have already discussed what happens when the giving or receiving action takes place between a member of the speaker's group and a member of the addressee's group. The third person in such a case is treated exactly the same as either the addressee or the speaker, depending on which group he is a member of. Thus the giving action between the speaker's mother and the addressee's daughter is expressed in the same way as between the speaker and addressee as we have seen in example (8) above. However, when the action does not involve in-group/out-group interaction, and takes place between two individuals, neither of whom belong to the speaker's group, or in the opposite case where both belong to the speaker's group, additional factors besides the direction and angle (upwards or downwards) need to be taken into consideration. We will refer to the giver and the receiver in such cases as third persons, even though one of them may be a member of the addressee's (second person's) group.

In the simpler cases discussed previously, the giving and receiving action places the speaker in the center in the two diagrams. When A gives something to B, but neither A nor B is a member of the speaker's group, or both of them are members of the speaker's family, one of the two must be put in the circle "I" in order to express the giving/receiving action. The factors to be considered in choosing between the two individuals are identification and proximity.

IDENTIFICATION

The person whom the speaker is identified with, or is psychologically closer to, is put in the circle for "I."

(10) "Kazuko-san had the letter translated by Yamanaka-san. (Kazuko-san received the favor of translating from Yamanaka-san.)"

    N: F: *Kazuko-san wa Yamanaka-san ni tegami o honyaku shite moratta no.*

The person the speaker refers to as Kazuko-san is obviously closer to the speaker. The fact that the speaker refers to her by the first name plus *-san* as opposed to the last name plus *-san* of Yamanaka-san suggests the closeness. If *Kazuko-san* is replaced by *Tanaka-san*, the verb *morau* becomes the only clue for Tanaka-san being closer to the speaker.

(11) "Suzuki Sensei loaned (gave the favor of loaning) a book to Murayama-san."

    P-1: *Suzuki Sensei wa Murayama-san ni hon o kashite kudasaimashita.*

Here Murayama-san is placed into the circle, and the arrow comes downward from Suzuki Sensei. The speaker is closer to Murayama-san, a fellow student, and is identified with him/her. Suppose the speaker is a fellow teacher of Suzuki Sensei. The same event would be reported differently.

(12) **P-0**: *Suzuki Sensei wa Murayama-san ni hon o kashite yarimashita.*

    P-1: *Suzuki Sensei wa Murayama-san ni hon o kashite oyari ni narimashita.*

The speaker here is identified with Suzuki Sensei and Suzuki Sensei is placed into the circle with the arrow going downwards away from the circle. The second sentence with the exalting *oyari ni naru* form may be assumed to have been uttered by a female teacher. It was mentioned earlier that women avoid using *yaru* these days, and replace it with *ageru*. The exalting form, *o-yari ni naru*, however, does not meet with this resistance.

Addressee with Third Person. Suppose the addressee is the giver or recipient in an interaction with a third person. In P-level speech, one always puts the addressee on a pedestal. If one puts the addressee in the center circle and uses verbs in the top part of the two diagrams, namely *sashiageru*, *itadaku*, and *kudasaru* in reference to the addressee, it would imply putting the addresseee below the partner in action, resulting in rudeness. **The safe way of referring to the addressee's giving and receiving action would be to use *o-age ni naru*, and *o-morai ni naru*,** but avoid the use of Set 3 verbs, *kudasaru* and *kureru*, for reasons to be explained later. Let us see what happens when one incorrectly uses the exalting or humling verbs for the addressee's action.

(13) "I understand that you gave two kittens to Yamada-san."
    P-1:**Yamada-san ni koneko o nihiki sashiageta soo desu ne.*
      (Incorrect)

The use of of the humbling verb *sashiageru* means "You gave upwards to Yamada-san," with the resulting implication that the addressee "you" is lower in status than Yamada-san. In other words, the statement puts the addressee down. The proper way to express the same idea is:

(13) **P-1**: *Yamada-san ni koneko o nihiki o-age ni natta*
      soo desu ne.
where *o-age ni natta* is an exalting verb, showing respect to the addressee.

In the case of Set 3 verbs, *kudasaru* would have the same rude implication of putting the addressee down when the addressee is the recipient. *Kureru*, on the other hand, sounds too unrefined and thus rude to use in reference to the addressee. One would therefore say, "You will receive (*o-morai ni naru*) from X" instead of "X will give (*kudasaru*) you" to avoid using the Set 3 verbs. One exception might be the following under special circumstances.

(14) "I hear that Yamamoto Sensei loaned (gave the favor of loaning) a book to your husband."

P-2: *Yamamoto Sensei ga otaku no goshujin ni hon o kashite kudasatta soo de gozaimasu ne.*

where Yamamoto Sensei is known not to let his books out of his library. In this particular situation, the addressee's husband and the speaker have been subjected to the same inconvenience of never being able to borrow Yamamoto Sensei's books. The addressee's husband thus belongs to the same group of people as the speaker in this respect, and is thus put in the circle of "my" group, resulting in the use of *kudasatta*, with Yamamoto Sensei having the higher status.

In N-level speech between intimates, such as between family members or close friends, whether an exalting verb is used when referring to a third person of higher status, such as Suzuki Sensei in (12) above, depends to a large extent on the feeling of the speaker towards Suzuki Sensei or the personal speech style of the speaker. We have already seen that some women use exalting and humbling terms in their N-level speech as a personal style. While older people tend to express respect by applying exalting terms, the trend among younger people today is not to use exalting terms for a third person as long as he or his close associates are not present as listeners. Suppose Murayama-san is a close friend of the family. A younger person is likely to state (11) as follows:

(15) N: *Suzuki Sensei wa Murayama-san ni hon o kashite kureta.*
while an older person would more likely use *kudasatta* instead of *kureta*, unless he does not like Suzuki Sensei.

Between Speaker's Family Members. When the two participants in the action are both members of the speaker's family, again one has to choose one of the two to be put into the circle. There is no rule that applies to all situations. In each situation, the speaker chooses the one with whom he feels psychologically closer to at the moment. Examples follow.

(16) "That thing is something that Oniisan (elder brother) bought for Yooko."

N: *Sore wa Onii-san ga Yooko ni katte kureta no.*

Here reference by name to Yooko makes it obvious that Yooko is either the younger sister or daughter of the speaker, and *kureta* indicates that the speaker feels closer to Yooko than to Onii-san in this context. However, the same speaker could say,

(17) "Oniisan, let Yooko use your bicycle. (Please give the favor of loaning the bicycle to Yooko.)"
N: *Onii-san, Yooko ni jitensha kashite yatte yo.*

Double Use. Sometimes donatory verbs are coupled to produce sentences like the following:

(18) "Oniisan, won't you loan (give me the favor of loaning) your bicycle to Yooko?"
N: *Onii-san, Yooko ni jitensha kashite yatte kurenai?*

There are two donatory verbs here, *yatte* and *kurenai*, used in succession. They do not function as a compound verb. Rather *yatte* is a donatory verb of the embedded sentence:

Oniisan ga Yooko ni jitensha o kashite yaru.
(Oniisan gives the favor to Yooko in loaning her his bicycle.)
-te kurenai? means "Won't you give me the favor of the action?" where the action refers to the embedded sentence. To put the whole sentence in natural English, it becomes:
"Oniisan, do me a favor and loan your bicycle to Yooko, won't you?"
The essential message of the sentence, therefore, is not much different from the following sentence, making use of a single donatory verb:

(19) "Oniisan, won't you loan (give the favor of loaning) your-bicycle to Yooko?"
N: *Onii-san, Yooko ni jitensha kashite kurenai?*

As example (18) indicates, when there are two donatory verbs in succession, it means that the second donatory verb refers to giving or receiving of the action of the embedded sentence (with the first donatory verb).

Sentences with double (and sometimes triple) donatory verbs occur more frequently at the N level. In more polite speech at the P level, the first donatory verb is substituted by a regular verb whenever possible.

(20) "Please accept this."
    N: M: *Kore moratte kure.*
       F: *Kore moratte kurenai?*
    P-0: *Kore uketotte kudasai.*
    P-1: ***Kore (o) o-uketori (ni natte) kudasai.***
    P-2: *Kore o dooka o-uketori (ni natte) itadakemasen*
         deshooka?

(21) "Please give this to Mr./Ms. Kato."
    N: M: *Kore Kato-san ni yatte kure.*
       F: *Kore Kato-san ni yatte (kurenai?)*
    P-0: *Kore Kato-san ni watashite kudasai.*
    P-1: ***Kore Kato-san ni o-watashi (ni natte) kudasaimasen***
        ka?
    P-2: *Kore Kato-san ni o-watashi itadakemasen deshoo ka?*

Note that in (20) at the P level, a Set 2 donatory verb *itadaku/morau* (to receive) is not used for the word "accept." The reason is that, on the one hand, *morau* is not polite to be applied to the addressee. On the other hand, to use *itadaku* would mean that the addressee receives from upwards, putting the speaker (who is the giver) above the addressee. Thus the neutral verb *uketoru* (to accept) is used in the exalting form *o-uketori* (*ni naru*) with just one donatory verb. (*Kudasai* is derived from *kudasaru*, and has the meaning of "Please do me the favor of," the P-O equivalent to *kure*.)

Similarly at P levels in (21), instead of a Set 1 donatory verb for "to give," the neutral verb *watasu* (to hand over) is used in its exalting form *o-watashi* (*ni naru*) in order to avoid placing Kato-san above the addressee by using *sashiageru*.

If the third person is lower in status than the addressee, the use of double donatory verbs at the P level poses no problem as the following example indicates:

(22) "Please tell him/her (my child) so."
    N: M: *Ano ko ni soo itte yatte kure.*
        F: *Ano ko ni soo itte yatte* (*kurenai?*)
    P-0: *Ano ko ni soo itte yatte kudasai.*
    P-1: ***Ano ko ni soo osshatte yatte kudasaimasen ka?***
    P-2: *Ano ko ni soo osshatte yatte itadakemasen ka?*

The earlier example in N, (18), can also be put in P because Yooko is clearly lower in status than Onii-san.

(23) *Onii-san, Yooko ni jitensha kashite yatte itadakemasen ka?*

where Onii-san is a brother-in-law, and thus spoken to at the P-1 level. *Kashite yaru* in the embedded sentence indicates that the speaker is identified with Onii-san in giving the favor to Yooko.

PROXIMITY

The person who is in spacial proximity, such as living in the same household, is placed in the circle. If we consider "identification" as psychological proximity, then the term "proximity" would cover both types of factors—psychological and geographical proximity. Suppose the elder sister of the speaker intends to give a blouse to the younger sister of the speaker, and the speaker informs the younger sister of the elder sister's intention.

(23) "Oneesan says she'll give you a blouse."
    N: *Onee-san ga anata ni burausu o ageru tte* (*itteru wa*).

Here the speaker is identified with the elder sister. If the elder sister, however, is living away from the household where the speaker and the younger sister live, the sentence will be:

(24) N: *Onee-san ga anata ni burausu o kureru tte.*

Translated into English, the two sentences are exactly the same. However, when we consult the diagrams, *ageru* is giving from "my" group outwards (Set 1), while *kureru* (Set 3) is giving by someone from outside towards "my" group. In (23), the speaker's identification is with the elder sister, while in (24), it is with the younger sister. The basis for identification with the younger sister in the second sentence is not so much a psychological one as one based on the fact that the elder sister has become an outsider who no longer lives in the same household.

The factor of residential proximity is not likely to enter except with family members, although it is conceivable that it could have a bearing on the situation when the partners involved in an action of giving or receiving are two friends of the speaker who are psychologically, but not geographically, equidistant to the speaker. If one lives in the same city, while the other lives in a foreign country, the principle of proximity is likely to apply in deciding which of the two is to be placed into the circle of "my" group.

Feeling of the Speaker

Among intimates at the N level of speech, where one discloses one's feeling much more freely, the speaker's feeling towards the partner in the giving and receiving interaction can be a factor in the choice of donatory verbs.

The Japanese claim that their rich vocabulary of emotion-related words best reflects the Japanese emphasis on emotion over reason or logic. As native speakers of the language, they do not seem to be aware that the grammar of their language is even more revealing of their emotional orientation than the vocabulary. The Japanese language is indeed rich in mechanisms that enable them to express their emotions in very subtle ways.

One way in which emotion is revealed is whether or not one opts to apply exalting terms to a third person who is not present at the scene. It was pointed out earlier that the application of respect words depends partly on the feeling the speaker has towards that person. Suppose you tell your close friend that you gave some advice to a third person. If you like the third person, you would say:

(25) "I told him so."
     N: M: *Ano hito ni soo itte ageta n da.*
        F: *Ano hito ni soo itte ageta no.*

While if you dislike him, you would say,

(26) N: M: *Aitsu ni soo itte yatta n da.*
        F: *Ano hito ni soo itte yatta no.*

The difference is in the choice of "give" verbs (Set 1), whether the favor of giving the advice was positive and thus upwards or horizontal (25), or negative and thus downwards (26). *Itte yaru* has the connotation of "telling someone off."

If the speaker is at the receiving end, and he welcomes or appreciates the giving action of the third person, he would say,

(27) "Yesterday Yamamoto-san was nice enough to come (gave me the favor of coming) to my place."
     N: *Kinoo Yamamoto-san ga kite kureta.*

but if Yamamoto-san is someone the speaker does not like, or Yamamoto-san came at an inopportune time, the speaker would put the sentence into the adversity passive (or suffering passive) and say,

(28) "I was subjected to Yamamoto-san coming yesterday."
     N: *Kinoo Yamamoto-san **ni** korareta n da.*
     P-0: *Kinoo Yamamoto-san **ni** koraremashite nee . . .*

Among an intimate circle of friends one can subtly express whether or not one appreciated an action carried out on one's behalf by the appropriate grammatical construction. In P speech, one may soften the subtly revealed feeling by leaving the sentence incomplete as in (28).

Refined Expression at P-1 and P-2: *-sasete itadaku*

The equivalent of the "Closed" sign at stores in Japan is often a sentence that reads:

(29) P-2: *Honjitsu wa kyuugyoo sasete itadakimasu.*

which just means "Closed Today," but is put in an extremely polite form. The literal meaning is, "Presuming on your permission, we are closed today," or "We trust that you permit us to be closed today," with the resultant meaning "We are taking the liberty to be closed today." *Saseru* means "to let do" or "to make one do." Combined with the donatory verb *itadaku*, the phrase *sasete itadaku* is a polite way of saying "I will do" with the additional meaning, "With your permission" or "Presuming on your permission."

To create this construction, one must first put the verb into the *-te* form (gerund) of the causative, and then attach *itadaku*. The causative is formed like the passive, namely *-asete* is attached to the stem of U-Verbs (verbs with consonant-ending stems, or strong verbs), and *-sasete* to the stem of RU-Verbs (verbs with vowel-ending stems, or weak verbs), as shown in Chart 14. *Itadaku* is then attached to the causative gerund.

Chart 14: Causative Gerunds

English	Dictionary Citation Form	Causative Gerund
U Verbs		
to say	*i-u*	*iw-ase-te*

English	Dictionary Citation Form	Causative Gerund
to meet	*a-u*	*aw-ase-te*
to buy	*ka-u*	*kaw-ase-te*
to think, feel	*omo-u*	*omow-ase-te*
to visit, to ask	*ukaga-u*	*ukagaw-ase-te*
to go	*ik-u*	*ik-ase-te*
to listen, ask	*kik-u*	*kik-ase-te*
to write	*kak-u*	*kak-ase-te*
to erase, turn off	*kes-u*	*kes-ase-te*
to depart	*tats-u*	*tat-ase-te*
to win	*kats-u*	*kat-ase-te*
to wait	*mats-u*	*mat-ase-te*
to read	*yom-u*	*yom-ase-te*
to drink	*nom-u*	*nom-ase-te*
to carry out, do	*yar-u*	*yar-ase-te*
to cut	*kir-u*	*kir-ase-te*
to take	*tor-u*	*tor-ase-te*

RU Verbs

to be (at a place)	*i-ru*	*i-sase-te*
to think	*kangae-ru*	*kangae-sase-te*
to get up	*oki-ru*	*oki-sase-te*
to put on (clothes)	*ki-ru*	*ki-sase-te*
to look at	*mi-ru*	*mi-sase-te*
		haiken sase-te
to borrow	*kari-ru*	*kari-sase-te*
to eat	*tabe-ru*	*tabe-sase-te*
to go to bed	*ne-ru*	*ne-sase-te*

Irregular Verbs

to come	*ku-ru*	*ko-sase-te*
to do	*su-ru*	*s-ase-te*

Sasete, the last on the list above, being the causative gerund of *suru*, is used with humbling verbs of the *o-___ suru* type as follows.

Neutral	Humbling Verb *o-____ suru*	Causative Gerund
kari-ru	*o-kari suru*	*o-kari sase-te*
ukaga-u	*o-ukagai suru*	*o-ukagai sase-te*
okur-u (to send)	*o-okuri suru*	*o-okuri sase-te*

In very polite speech at P-1 or P-2 level, this form is frequently used, particularly in speaking to a person of higher status in a hier-archical relationship. For instance, the answer in P-2 to (1) "Did you read the book I gave you the other day?" would be:

(30) "Yes, I read it."
    P-1 & 2: *Hai, yomasete itadakimashita.*

in contrast to straight answers at lower levels of speech:
    N: M: *Un, yonda yo.*
       F: *Ee, yonda wa.*
    P-0: *Ee, yomimashita.*

The question "May I?" addressed to a higher-status person, or an out-group member, is often put in this form with *itadaku* in the potential form *itadakeru*. The literal meaning of such a phrase is, "Would (*deshoo*) it be possible for me to receive your permission to . . . ?" Examples follow.

(31) "May I visit you?"
    P-1: *O-ukagai shite mo yoroshii deshoo ka?*
    P-2: *O-ukagai sasete itadakemasu ka?*
        O-ukagai sasete itadakemasen deshoo ka?

(32) "May I come along?"
    P-0: *Issho ni itte mo ii desu ka?*
    P-1: ***Issho ni ikasete itadakemasu ka?***
    P-2: *Goissho sasete itadakemasen deshoo ka?*

As was pointed out in the chapter on levels, a request in the negative is more polite than one in the positive, and a non-affirmative sentence (*deshoo*) is more polite than an affirmative one. Even within this format of *sasete itadaku*, a number of gradations is possible. The following is in ascending order of politeness.

(33) "May I have a look at it?"
    P-0: *Misete moraemasu ka?*
          Misete moraemasen ka?
    P-1: ***Misete itadakemasu ka?***
          Misete itadakemasen ka?
    P-2: *Haiken sasete itadakemasu ka?*
          Haiken sasete itadakemasen ka?
          Haiken sasete itadakemasu deshoo ka?
          Haiken sasete itadakemasen deshoo ka?

Even though donatory verbs of Set 2 are used in all the sentences, the verb *misete* ("to show") is not in the causative (*s*)*asete* form. The P-0 and P-1 sentences, therefore, do not contain the meaning "with your permission." The donatory verbs, however, are in the potential form (*itadake-*, *morae-* above) with the meaning, "is it possible" (to receive the favor of your showing it to me), and thus is more polite than the straight request *Misete kudasai* ("Please show me").

Choodai Suru

There is one additional donatory verb—*choodai suru*—that has two meanings: one is "(I) receive," and the other is "give me."

When used in the form *choodai suru*, it is a humbling verb with the same meaning as *itadaku* of Set 2, except that it can be used only for receiving material objects and not for favors.

(30) "If you insist, I'll gratefully accept it."
     N: F+: *Sore nara, arigataku choodai suru wa yo.*
       P-1: ***Soo ossharu n deshitara, arigataku itadakimasu.***
          Soo ossharu n deshitara, arigataku choodai shimasu.
          Soo ossharu no deshitara, arigataku choodai
          itashimasu.
       P-2: *Soo osshàrareru no deshitara, arigataku choodai*
          sasete itadakimasu.

The sentences above are in ascending order of politeness, except for the first two P-1 sentences, which are exactly at the same level. If *choodai* in the refined P-2 sentence is replaced by *itadaku*, it becomes *itadakasete itadakimasu*, which is grammatically acceptable, but stylistically awkward.

The other meaning of *choodai* is equivalent to *kudasai*, but not as polite, for it is used only in N-level speech. Its use is limited to making a request, whether for material objects or favors, or giving an order as follows:

(31) "Please give it to me."
     N: *Sore choodai yo.*
       Choodai!

(32) "Go to the post office and get me ten postcards, will you?"
     N: *Yuubinkyoku e itte, hagaki juu-mai katte kite choodai?*

It is interesting that the same word is used with different meanings in such contrasting ways: one used mostly at P levels in a humble way, while the other is used only at the N level in a commanding way. The word *choodai*, however, is used frequently enough to merit inclusion in this chapter.

Summary Guide

The donatory verbs are the most complex part of the Japanese

honorific language system. Yet because of their frequent usage, one cannot pretend complete ignorance of them when one speaks Japanese. In order not to insult the addressee, the following are suggested for a minimum level of competence:

1. Memorize the diagrams: the directions and angles of the arrows with the verbs in all three sets.

2. Remember the in-group/out-group principle.

3. At the P levels of speech, use the verbs in the upper part of the diagrams for giving to and receiving from the addressee and members of his group.

4. Use the verbs from the lower halves of the diagrams in reporting to an out-group person the giving and receiving actions within your own family.

If you have Japanese relatives, familiarize yourself with the section on giving and receiving among third persons. When you feel comfortable enough with the minimum level of competence outlined above, you can try to express yourself in the *-sasete itadaku* form. While that form is not difficult to master, a foreigner who can use it is likely to be assumed to have an excellent mastery of the honorific system, and thus is less likely to be excused for making more basic mistakes in politeness expression. It is therefore suggested that other aspects be put under control first.

7. Review of Levels

We have covered all the relevant parts of speech that have *keigo* words. Through the sample sentences, you already have a rough idea of how they relate to levels of speech. One should not mix levels, that is use a formal P-2-level word at the N level of speech and vice versa. There are restrictions as to what can co-occur with what. In this chapter, we will put all the separate parts together to obtain cohesiveness at each level, and discuss which level to use when.

Minimum Politeness: P-1 Speech

The emphasis of this book is on basic or minimum essential politeness to the addressee, which means the P-1 level of speech. While **a sentence at the P-1 level must have cohesion, and use concurrently all that is essential to show respect to the addressee**, we will review the essential components in order of importance. When you have not yet mastered all the components of polite speech, expressions to show respect to the addressee are more important and therefore must come first, before those expressing humility of self. You should, however, aim at mastering all the components in order to achieve cohesion in P-1-level speech.

ESSENTIAL COMPONENTS OF P-1 IN ORDER OF IMPORTANCE

desu/-masu. The first and most important step to polite speech is the sentence ending *desu/-masu* (and derivatives). Sentences that end in verb phrases without *desu/-masu* are in the nonpolite or plain style, namely at the N level. If you remember that N-level speech is used downwards to speak to lower-status persons in a power relationship, or exchanged mutually between intimate equals, you can immediately see how insulting it is to use N-level speech in speaking to someone who is not an intimate friend nor a subordinate.

Title, or LN-*san*, and Non-Use of *anata*. *Anata* is absolutely taboo, and in its place, either the addressee's title or his last name with -*san* must be used.

Exalting Verbs. The use of exalting verbs for actions of the addressee (and members of his group) is essential to show respect. Starting with the lexical substitutes of frequently used verbs, such as *irassharu* and *ossharu*, and then using the *o-___ ni naru* form or the infix -*are-/-rare-* for other verbs, one should eventually put every verb related to the action of the addressee in the exalting form.

Honorific Prefix for Nouns. For nouns relating to the addressee, the *o-* or *go-* prefix must be attached. Women must also attach the *o-* prefix to a large number of nouns commonly related to daily life regardless of the level of speech. Men must also do so at the P-1 level.

Kinship Terms. The differentiation in the use of the neutral humbling form of kinship terms for one's own family members and the exalting ones for those of others must be mastered for all levels of speech, including the N level. Non-native speakers as well as native speakers tend to be more familiar with the exalting forms than the humbling forms, because the exalting forms are used also to address one's own family members. However, the use of an exalting form such as *o-too-san* to refer to one's own family member is associated with immaturity and lack of education. For this reason, one should try to master the humble forms, beginning with those used for immediate family members.

Donatory Verbs. The use of donatory verbs is not restricted to the P levels of speech. However, the use of the upper half of each set of donatory verbs (*sashiageru*, *o-age suru*, *itadaku*, and *kudasaru*) for in-group/out-group interaction, and the lower half (*yaru*, *morau*, and *kureru*) for reporting in-group interaction is essential at the P-1 level and above.

Humbling Verbs. Humbling verbs need not be used for every action of the speaker (and members of the speaker's group), except those actions expressed by humbling lexical substitutes, such as *oru*, *itasu*, *mairu*, etc. The *o-___ suru* form is used mainly when an action is carried out on behalf of the addressee and members of his group.

Refined Set of Demonstratives. Words with *ko-*, *so-*, *a-*, *do-* should be replaced by the refined version *kochira*, *sochira*, *achira*, *dochira*, and *ikaga* whenever possible. Similarly *kata* should be used instead of *hito*.

P-2 Speech

The P-2 level is often referred to as the ultra-polite level, but it is also the most formal speech, used by Diet members, for instance, when addressing the Diet.

The P-2 level of speech is called the *gozaimasu* style in Japan in contrast to the *desu/-masu* style of P-0 to P-1. The word *gozaimasu* is selected just to characterize and represent this highest level of polite speech. As the many sample sentences at the P-2 level indicate, not all sentences end in *gozaimasu*. It is mainly the presence of Chinese compounds, and the use of exalting and humbling words wherever possible, that make the P-2 level more polite than the P-1 level. Exalting words are used not only for the addressee but for the third person as well. When these distinguishing characteristics are lacking, however, such as in a neutral statement that does not end in *desu* (e.g., "The semester is already over" *Gakki wa moo owarimashita*), a sentence uttered in P-2-level speech may not be much different from a P-1 sentence.

Today there is not much need for P-2-level speech except in particular settings that demand extreme formality or politeness, such as in the Diet, or in sales talk. Some women from better families, educated before the end of the war, tend to speak at the P-2 level to anyone who is not intimate. Hence, it is desirable to have at least passive comprehension of P-2-level speech.

CHARACTERISTIC COMPONENTS OF P-2

All P-1 Components. All the components mentioned earlier for the P-1 level must be present in the P-2 level. In addition to these, the following components characterize P-2-level speech.

Use of Chinese Compounds. The commonly used adverbs of time, such as *ima*, *kyoo*, and *kyonen*, are words of Japanese origin. These adverbs, which function also as nouns, are usually replaced by Chinese compounds with the *on* reading at the P-2 level. A sampling is given in Chart 15.

There are many other Chinese compounds used for formality in writing. The etiquette of writing letters, however, requires a book in itself. Here we are concerned only with speech.

Articulation of Post-Position Particles. Particles such as *wa*, *ga*, and *o* may be occasionally omitted in P-1 speech, but at the P-2 level, every particle is articulated. Similarly contractions are avoided at this level of speech.

gozaimasu. The *desu* (and its derivatives) in P-0 and P-1 sentences is replaced by *de gozaimasu* in P-2. Thus *Kiree desu* becomes

Chart 15: Chinese Compounds Used at the P-2 Level

English	Japanese Words	Chinese Compounds
today	*kyoo*	*honjitsu*
yesterday	*kinoo*	*sakujitsu*
the day before yesterday	*ototoi*	*issakujitsu*
tomorrow	*ashita*	*myoonichi*
the day after tomorrow	*asatte*	*myoogonichi*
the other day	*kono aida*	*senjitsu*
this year	*kotoshi*	*honnen*
last year	*kyonen*	*sakunen*
the year before last	*ototoshi*	*issakunen*
next year	*rainen*	*myoonen*
the year after next	*sarainen*	*myoogonen*
"you all"	*mina-san*	*go-ichidoo-sama*

Kiree de gozaimasu, Sore wa kinoo deshita becomes *Sore wa sakujitu de gozaimashita, Taihen datta deshoo* becomes *Taihen de gozaimashita deshoo, Omoshiroku nakatta n desu* becomes *Omoshiroku nakatta no de gozaimasu.* Similarly *arimasu* is changed to *gozaimasu* as in *Soo de wa gozaimasen deshita* for *Soo ja arimasen deshita.*

The Use of *-asete/-sasete itadakimasu*. As an extra-humble expression of one's action in relation to the addressee, *sasete itadaku* is frequently used at the P-2 level, where humble expressions must be used whenever possible.

***-are-/-rare-* as the Preferred Exalting Form**. When P-2-level speech is used in a formal address or lecture, it is "formality" rather than "respect" that is called for. In such a situation, of the two available grammatical devices to create exalting verbs, the *-are-/-rare-* form is considered to be more appropriate. The *o-___*

ni naru form is perceived to be more "polite," while the *-are-/-rare-* form more "formal."

N Speech

CHARACTERISTICS OF N-LEVEL SPEECH

Since N-level speech is limited to the inner circle of friends and family members, or used in speaking down to a lower-status person, expression of respect through exalting and humbling terms is not necessary. As was pointed out earlier, some women do use these respect terms in N-level speech, not so much as a sign of respect for the addressee but more as a matter of personal speech style.

There are other components of the P-1 and P-2 levels that are not appropriate in N-level speech. Cohesion in N-level speech means not using these characteristic "respect" forms. The exceptions are those that apply to all levels of speech, namely: *o-* prefix by women for commonly used nouns; the honorific suffix (*-san*, *-kun*) after FN or LN; and the humble and exalting kinship terms for one's own and someone else's family members, respectively.

Characteristics of N-level speech which are usually not permissible at the P levels are: the use of second person pronouns *anata* and *kimi*; omission of post-position particles *wa* and *o* when understood; the use of sentence particles *yo*, *wa*, *zo*, *ne*, *na*, etc., most of which are gender specific; and the use of contractions (e.g., *kaiteru* for *kaite iru*). Because N-level speech is not the concern of this book, such "contraction" has appeared only in some of the N-level sample sentences.

Summary

The characteristic components of the various levels of speech are summarized in Chart 16. The chart shows that some components are shared across all levels, while others are used only in certain levels. The order in which the components are listed does not coincide with the order of importance in which they were presented in this chapter.

Chart 16: Characteristic Components of Various Levels of Speech

Characteristics	N	P-0	P-1	P-2
gozaimasu	-	-	-	+
Chinese Compounds	-	-	-	+
Articulation of Post-Position Particles	-	-	-	+
sasete itadakimasu	-	-	-	+
Exalting Verbs for a Third Person	-	-	-	+
Upper Half of Donatory Verb Sets	-	-	+	+
Title in Address	-	-	+	+
Exalting Verbs	-	-	+	+
Humbling Verbs	-	-	+	+
Exalting Nouns with *o-/go-*	-	-	+	+
Refined Demonstratives	-	-	+	+
desu/-masu	-	+	+	+
Two Sets of Kinship Terms	+	+	+	+
Use of Donatory Verbs	+	+	+	+
LN-*san*	+	+	+	+
FN-*san*	+	+	+	-
anata/kimi	+	+	-	-
Omission of Sentence Particles	+	-	-	-
Contractions	+	-	-	-

The chart indicates only general usage. It should be pointed out that there are always some minor exceptions. For instance, a person who uses P-2-level speech indiscriminately to any out-group person is more likely to use sentence particles like *yo* or *ne* to express emphasis or assurance than a person who uses P-2-level speech only on formal occasions.

Which Level to Use When

The *keigo* system is an essential part of the Japanese language, and *keigo* words, which are elements or components of that system, play an important role. Not to use *keigo* would be like using only *tu* in French, Spanish, or Italian; or using only *du* in German. The offensiveness of being spoken to in that way may be more easily comprehensible to those who speak one of the European languages that makes a similar distinction, and harder to grasp for English-speaking people, particularly Americans (see Appendix). This may be the reason why so many Americans who are otherwise knowledgeable about things Japanese choose to ignore the *keigo* system. As was mentioned before, grammatical mistakes by foreigners are easily ignored, but rudeness stemming from non-use of *keigo* may not always be forgiven.

Even in American English, the inclusion of the word "please" does not necessarily make the sentence very polite. "Please make ten copies of this paper" is nothing but a polite command, and one would not utter such a sentence even to one's friend, unless the friend has agreed to assist one in one's deadline work, and is standing by to receive orders.

Similarly, *Kore ashita made ni shite oite kudasai* ("Please have this finished by tomorrow") can be said only to one's subordinate. Even though it is in P, it is a polite command at the P-0 level. When speaking to an equal-status person, such as a friend, one should put it in the form of a question just as one would in English, using "Will you . . . ?" or "Could you . . . ?" In Japanese, one should also use a donatory verb, and put the question in the more polite negative form. The request in N to a close friend can be made in the following ways, given in the order of less polite to more polite:

(1) "Will you do me the favor of finishing this by tomorrow?"
   N: *Kore ashita made ni shite oite kurenai?*
   Kore ashita made ni shite oite kudasaranai?
   Kore ashita made ni shite oite itadakenai?

As you will remember, *kudasaru* is the exalting equivalent of *kureru* (someone gives me or to a member of my group); while *itadaku* is the humbling equivalent of *morau* (I or a member of my group receives). Note that *itadakenai* is in the potential, having the literal meaning of "May I (is it possible for me to) receive?" and thus is more polite than *kudasaranai*. To make the same request at the P-1 level, all one needs to do is to change the last donatory verb into the *-masu* form with the question particle *ka*, such as *kuremasen ka, kudasaimasen ka*, and *itadakemasen ka*.

The status conscious Japanese, as pointed out earlier, is extremely sensitive to how he is spoken to. If he feels you have given him an order, spoken to him in N when he is not your subordinate, or spoken to him in familiar terms when he is not an intimate equal of yours, he may take your words as an intentional insult. The immediate reaction is an emotional response not under rational control. Words can cut as deeply as a sword. Yet few Americans seem to be aware of the effect their speech can have on the Japanese addressee.

The following is a review on status relationships and the concomitant level of speech for each.

HIGHER-STATUS INDIVIDUALS: P-1

The general term used to refer to a higher-status person is *meue*. A *meue* is any person who is older, who has been working in the same place longer, or who holds a higher position than you. Such people must be spoken to in P-1, while they are entitled to speak to you in N. Be careful not to misinterpret the N-level speech by the other person as the mutual N of intimacy. When there is a status difference, the level of speech is non-reciprocal, and the lower-status person must speak in P, while the higher-status person may speak in N, although he or she may choose to speak in P-0.

The following *meue* people should be given particular respect.

Benefactor. Any official of a company, agency, or school who helps you obtain the visa to come to Japan, or who hires you, or who helps or will help you in your research or work, even if he is younger than you, should be treated as a benefactor (to whom you are obligated and owe *giri*), and thus a *meue* person. The P-1 level of speech must be used in speaking to such a person.

Teacher. Any teacher from whom you receive lessons or instructions must be addressed as *sensei* and given respect in speech (P-1 level) and behavior. Only if you exchange language lessons, where each is the teacher in one language and student in the other, can you do away with the *sensei* title.

Doctor, Dentist, Lawyer. Any individual who provides you professional service is *meue* to you, and you must speak to him accordingly at the P-1 level.

Your Host Family Parents. If you are a high school student or an undergraduate in college, and you are treated as one of the host family's children, then you might speak to your host parents the same way as their children do, namely in N. However, if you are a graduate student, or are over 25, you are expected to speak at the P-1 level to your host parents. This is particularly true when you have a regular job in Japan or your home country, and are considered to be a *shakaijin*, a responsible adult citizen. As such, you should no longer speak and behave like a student. If you speak any Japanese at all, you will be expected to be sufficiently knowledgable about the Japanese culture to observe the rules of showing respect to anyone higher in status. You should, therefore, speak in the P-1 style to the host parents, using the proper address terms (*otoo-san*, *okaa-san*, but *sensei* if the host father is a professional). Only to those in the family who are the same age as you or younger may you speak in N. If, however, you are reunited with former host parents whom you spoke to at the N level in the past, you may continue to use N-level speech no matter how old you have become.

Sempai. If you attend a school or university in Japan as a regular student or work in a Japanese company, you will have *sempai*. A *sempai* is a *meue* (senior) person who at some point in your life has been or is currently a member of the same group. He may have attended the same school as you—his *koohai*—or he may work at the same place or belong to the same professional organization. In any event, he has joined the organization or school one or more years before you. Although all those ahead of you in the same organization are your *sempai*, you may develop an especially close relationship with one particular *sempai*, and he may become like a mentor to you. In such a special relationship, called the **sempai-koohai relationship**, your *sempai* may look after your welfare in your work as well as personal life, find a marriage partner for you, or help you land a job. He serves as your benefactor. Obviously, one must use P-1-level speech to a *sempai*.

The doing of favors is not one-way from *sempai* to *koohai*, but also from *koohai* to *sempai*. A *koohai* is expected to do menial jobs for his *sempai*, such as provide help in moving or assist at a family funeral. The *koohai* sends a gift to his *sempai* twice annually, as *o-chuugen* in early July, and *o-seibo* at the end of the year. A non-Japanese generally need not do so during his first years in Japan, but he certainly would be expected to follow such customs as he becomes more familiar with life in Japan, particularly if he works semi-permanently among the Japanese for a Japanese company, or has married into a Japanese family.

INDIVIDUALS IN LONG-TERM NON-INTIMATE RELATIONS: MUTUAL P-1

In Japan, if one starts out a relationship with an individual (such as a neighbor) at the P level of speech, the speech level remains the same throughout the association, no matter how long it becomes. **Generally one either starts with N-level speech from the very beginning, or speaks consistently at a P level with a particular individual. In normal circumstances, long associations do not lead to lowering the speech level from the polite P to an intimate N.** An "intimate" in Japan, therefore, means someone you knew from childhood, when you could speak only N-level speech, a classmate in school, or an equal at work. Remember that in Japan, the category of "equal" is very narrow, and does not include someone who is even one year your senior in school or at work.

For these reasons, the category of non-intimate friends is rather broad in Japan. The individuals in this category are essentially "out-group" people, whom you treat as if they had higher status than you, based on the **in-group/out-group principle**.

Non-Intimate Friends. Someone whom Europeans would classify as an "acquaintance" and with whom you are not on very intimate terms, such as a neighbor, would be spoken to in P-1. The use of P-1-level speech is mutual.

INDIVIDUALS IN BRIEF IMPERSONAL INTERACTIONS: P-1, P-0, OR N

In brief impersonal interactions with individuals, such as at ticket counters, hotel front desks, banks, and post offices, speech level is determined by the speaker's sex and personality as well as by the specific situation. When one asks a favor, such as for assistance or information, one takes a low posture and speaks at a higher level of speech than when providing information or requesting for things one is entitled to (such as a ticket at the ticket counter). Women generally speak at a slightly higher level than men.

Service Personnel at Banks, Post Offices, Government Offices, Train Stations. In these situations it is best to use the P-0 level, which means the use of no *keigo* words other than the *desu/-masu* sentence ending. Some men, however, use N, and are often resented for their arrogance. In requesting a loan at the bank, or a visa extension at an immigration office, one can expect more cordial treatment if one uses P-1-level speech.

Service Personnel at Commercial Establishments. At restaurants, hotels, and stores, the customer (*okyaku-san*) is treated as a higher-status person. Men usually use N, women P-0, but there is no strict rule.

Taxi Driver. Men usually use N, while women use P-0 or N. It should be mentioned that many taxi drivers these days do not treat the passenger as a "customer," who has the higher status, but act as if they are doing a favor for the customer. In situations like this, it is generally more effective to use polite P-level speech than respond at the same N-level. Remember that P-level speech creates a distance between the speaker and addressee.

Policeman or Stranger: for Directions. Since you are asking for assistance in this situation, you do not use N-level speech. Men tend to use P-0 and women P-1.

A Complete Stranger. In responding to a request for information by a stranger, or calling on a complete stranger to let him know that he dropped something in a "one-time-only encounter," one can use the P-0 level of speech. Women tend to use P-1. It is up to the individual to choose the level of speech.

INTIMATE CIRCLES: N

The Japanese seem to feel completely at ease only in intimate circles, where mutual N is exchanged. Some feel that they can be informal with foreigners and open up to them, probably a case of "strangers on the train" phenomenon. You have to play it by ear and if they speak to you in N, you can respond to them in N also, as long as it is not a hierarchical relationship. Individuals with whom you can exchange mutual N are listed below.

Intimate Equals. Strictly speaking, only your classmates in school from kindergarten to college, and those who started working at the same place at the same time, are equals, with whom you can exchange mutual N from the very beginning. Others about the same age who were strangers at first, but with whom you have become intimate over a period of time, can be considered intimate equals. Let the other person, however, take the initiative to exchange mutual N. Those who are one year ahead of you in school or at your workplace are *sempai*, and must be spoken to in P-1, with respect.

Host Family Members. If you are taken into a host family while you are still in your teens, you can speak to every member of the family in N as do regular Japanese family members.

LOWER STATUS INDIVIDUALS: P-0 OR N

Lower-status individuals are referred to as ***meshita***. Someone definitely younger, or junior in rank, or newer at your place of work is a *meshita*, a lower-status person. One can address a *meshita* in non-reciprocal N, which means that the *meshita* has to respond in P-1 as is appropriate in a *meue/meshita* hierarchical relationship. Women generally choose to speak in P-0 to *meshita* except to children and domestic help. This tendency, however, seems to be breaking down as women occupy executive positions and take on roles formerly assigned only to men.

Your Subordinate or Assistant. Those working under you are definitely *meshita* and may be spoken to in N. Men usually use N to a person just one year their junior to assert their senior status, while women tend to use P-0. It appears that N-level speech commands greater authority.

Your Student or Pupil. If you teach, your students and pupils are *meshita*, and can be spoken to in N. If, however, you teach an adult class, or give private lessons to an adult, it is better not to treat your students as *meshita*. In such a situation, it is best to use minimally P-0-level speech.

Your Clients. If you are a professional (doctor, lawyer, consultant, etc.), your patients, clients or customers will consider you their *meue*. This does not necessarily mean that you should treat them as your *meshita*. It is best to speak to them in the same way as a teacher would to an adult student, namely minimally at P-0, and possibly at P-1.

Children. Children are always spoken to in N, without the use of pronouns "I" and "you" as discussed in Chapter 5.

Summary

The rule is strict on how one speaks to a person who is of higher status or whom one owes favors to, or to an out-group person, but more flexible when it comes to speaking to anyone else. Where there is freedom of choice, the speaker's sex, upbringing, and personality tend to be the determining factors.

Men tend to use N whenever permissible. Adult women speak more politely than men, which means they tend to speak at one level higher. The majority of adult women speak in N only to family members, close friends, children, and household help. The higher-status person has a choice in speaking to his *meshita* in either N or P-0, but the *meshita* person must use at least P-1 to the higher-status person, since the level of speech is not reciprocal in a hierarchical relationship.

8. Current Trends

Foreigners are not the only people who have to struggle to master *keigo*. The younger people in Japan today are only slightly ahead of the non-native speaker when they begin using *keigo* as they enter adulthood. The advantages they have over the non-native speaker are merely that they have had passive exposure to it and that they are more sensitive to status differences. Unless they have worked part-time at a job involving contact with customers, they have had relatively little practice in using *keigo* themselves.

Current Condition with Regard to *Keigo*

In prewar days the growing child received guidance in the use of *keigo* at home and at school. But with the democratization of the teacher-student relationship, where the teacher plays the role of friend to the students, students no longer use *keigo* in speaking to their teachers. At home, too, in a small nuclear family where the father is absent for much of the children's waking hours, hierarchy is hardly observed. In today's two-child families, girls and boys receive the same treatment at home, unlike in the days when the average family had five or more children. In such a large family, boys had greater personal freedom and more privileges, while girls learned not only to share in all the household chores, but also to speak like a woman with the use of proper *keigo*. The girl who attends a coeducational school today not only picks up male speech but often does not receive much correction of her speech at home either. Only if the student works part-time or belongs to a sports club is he or she forced to use *keigo*. Sports clubs are known for their strict enforcement of hierarchical order, and students who speak in N to their teachers must speak in P to members who are merely one year their senior. In general, the growing child manages to get along without the use of *keigo*, except the *desu/-masu* ending (P-0 level) in answering questions in the classroom.

The great number of younger people from the countryside who flock to large cities for employment also have problems in that they are not familiar with the *keigo* of the standard dialect spoken in the metropolitan areas. Large companies faced with *keigo* illiterates are forced to provide training in the use of *keigo* during the orientation period for their new employees.

The fact that many of the younger people acquire *keigo* in their early twenties, much like a second language, means that they fumble and make many mistakes in the early stages. Their job may require speaking to the public or to customers—as a tour guide, receptionist, or sales clerk. Hence the public is exposed to misused *keigo* all the time.

The result of all this is "the confused state of *keigo*" or *keigo no midare* as the Japanese refer to it in their outcry. It appears that the more confusion there is, the greater the effort to train the young in *keigo*. *Keigo* is considered to be the lubricant that enables human interactions to run smoothly in this crowded country, and there is little likelihood that *keigo* will be done away with. An adult is expected to be able to handle *keigo*. One who is not able to speak *keigo* properly is much like a person who does not speak the official or standard language of his country and can function only in his dialect. His linguistic handicap shuts him out from the prospect of promotion to more important positions.

New Trends

The *keigo* system as a whole as well as its parts has changed over the centuries, and continues to change. In the years after World War II, an effort towards simplification was made by the Ministry of Education in the form of recommendations entitled "*Kore kara no keigo*" (1952), drafted by a group of scholars. Change in speech, however, cannot be achieved simply by a government recommendation in the same manner as it can be in orthography. In areas where the authorities have greater influence, such as in education, civil service, and news reporting through the cooperation of journalists, some simplification has been achieved. For instance, the use of special vocabulary reserved for the Emperor and the royal family has been done away with. Orders in the imperative form from the government to citizens or teachers to students, such as instructions on various application and registration forms or examinations, have been replaced by more polite statements or requests. The effort in these areas towards simplification has been directed towards the general use of the medium level of politeness in a wide range of circumstances, discouraging, but not forbidding, the use of the extremely polite level as well as the speaking downwards to lower-status individuals.

Many of the recommendations, however, went unheeded. For instance, it was recommended that *anata* be used as the polite second person pronoun, but obviously it was too late to rescue the word *anata* from its fallen state. The recommendation to speak politely downwards, not just upwards, has also been ignored. The idea behind this particular recommendation was to stress respect for the other human being regardless of status in an effort towards democratization and equalization in human relationships. This could be interpreted as recommending a switch from the hierarchy-based use of *keigo* to an intimacy-based use. This already is the trend in Europe, where both V (the P in Japanese) and T (the N in Japanese) are used mutually on the basis of degree of intimacy, and the non-reciprocal use of V and T on the basis of hierarchy is going out of style (see Appendix).

Japan seems to go counter to the general trend in democratic societies. There is no sign that the observation of hierarchy is becoming lax. The status-conscious Japanese are not likely to give up their prerogative to be spoken up to by lower-status individuals and to speak down to them, for these are symbols of status. Hierarchy, in fact, seems to be observed more strictly and earlier in one's life today than in prewar days. For instance, the word *sempai* was not used as an address term before World War II, but today's high school students address their seniors as *sempai*. The in-group/out-group distinction, essential in the use of *keigo* and a reflection of the strong group orientation of the Japanese, also has become sharper after the war, particularly at the workplace, a result of the *keigo* training given new employees. There is little indication of a relaxation in the use of *keigo*.

There are, however, some changes. The most noticeable change is the non-use of *keigo* (mainly *sonkei-go*, the exalting terms) in reference to a third person who is not present at the scene as a listener and who is unrelated to the addressee. (If the third person is a member of the addressee's group, the in-group/out-group principle is still observed, and he or she will be referred to with exalting terms.) One of the unique aspects of the Japanese *keigo* system— that *keigo* is applied not only to the addressee, but also to a third person who is the topic of the conversation—is thus disappearing. In this respect *keigo* is becoming more addressee oriented.

Another change that has resulted from *keigo* confusion on the one hand, and emphasis on *keigo* on the other, is the overuse of *keigo* by some. This is particularly the case with sales clerks and in bank advertisements. Sales clerks of large department stores, who use P-2-level speech to their customers, are for this reason not necessarily good models of *keigo* usage.

Similarly, there is a trend to use exalting or humbling terms in places where they are uncalled-for in an effort to be polite and to appear sophisticated. The result is for some of the exalting and humbling terms to be used purely for "refinement." This trend is expected to continue.

Despite all the confusion and mess created by the younger

shakaijin (responsible adult citizens) who are forced to use *keigo* before they have fully acquired it, *keigo* is here to stay. It is hard to imagine a Japanese society without *keigo*. As long as the society is hierarchically oriented, and group identity remains strong, the rules of *keigo* are not likely to change. One might as well face the reality that there is no escape from *keigo* when one speaks Japanese.

The foreigner may find solace in the fact that even native speakers of Japanese have problems with *keigo* and that many are trying to acquire it after they reach adulthood. However, the native speaker does eventually master the level appropriate to his job or social position. The foreigner should do so as well, especially in view of the fact that *keigo* appears to be growing progressively stricter. Don't forget that showing respect through polite speech and behavior to the non-intimate addressee is the most important aspect of human relationships in Japan. Now that you have started down the path toward good *keigo* use, keep going until you have mastered at least the minimum essential level. Far from being perceived as an arrogant foreigner, you will be respected as an associate who has made an effort to learn about the Japanese people.

APPENDIX: The Keigo System in Relation to the European V/T System

Japanese is not the only language with a system to express politeness and respect. In practically all languages in the world, there are ways of speaking politely and formally in contrast to speaking familiarly and informally. The linguistic device by which politeness is expressed, however, varies from language to language.

The V/T System in European Languages

In most European languages, there are two second person pronouns coming from the Latin *tu* and *voi*: namely *tu* and *vous* in French, *tu* and *vos* (later *usted*) in Spanish; *tu* and *voi* (now *lei*) in Italian; *du* and *Sie* (originally *Ihr*) in German. English also had *thou* and *ye*, but *thou* is no longer used except in prayers, and *ye* has become *you*. Brown and Gilman in an article entitled "The Pronouns of Power and Solidarity," which has become a classic in sociolinguistics, use T as a generic symbol to represent the former of all these pairs, namely the familiar second person pronoun, and V for the latter, the polite second person pronoun.

They point out that two semantic dimensions are involved in the use of these pronouns today: the **power semantic between the superior and the inferior that is asymmetrical; and the solidarity semantic where intimacy or non-intimacy is symmetrical between the speaker and the addressee.**

The person who has the greater power based on wealth, age, sex, physical strength, or institutionalized role in the church, in the state, in the army, or within the family, is the superior. In medieval Europe and for some time beyond, the superior spoke in T to the inferior, and received V in return. Such superior/inferior discourse occurred between nobility and common people, masters and slaves or subordinates, and parents and children. Equals of the upper class exchanged mutual V, while equals of the lower classes exchanged mutual T. In later centuries, the extensive use of V, being associated with the upper class, became a mark of elegance.

A gradual change, however, set in. Among equals, social class membership originally determined whether the mutual V or mutual T was used. This gradually gave way to an emphasis on intimacy, the solidarity dimension, where mutual T came to be exchanged among intimates, and mutual V among non-intimates. The solidarity dimension appears to be winning out over the power dimension as the governing principle for the choice of V or T today. The basis for mutual T apparently is gradually expanding and mutual T is being used these days among fellow students, fellow workers, members of the same political group, or among people who have shared a common task or common fate, with some variations in different countries. It should be emphasized, however, that the two dimensions do coexist, resulting in the common definition of **T as the pronoun of either condescension or intimacy, and V as the pronoun of reverence or formality.**

When a person has been using V consistently to another, and suddenly switches to T, this momentary shift expresses his change in mood. If the V has been that of reverence, then the switch suggests that the speaker treats the addressee at that particular point as an inferior. If it has been that of formality or distance, then the speaker temporarily treats the adressee as an intimate. Similar interpretation applies to a sudden switch from T to V. Brown and Gilman cite a number of interesting cases of temporary switch from V to T as well as T to V found in European literature. Such sudden shifts—breaking of the customary norm—in the use of the second person pronoun is an extremely effective way to express a temporary mood like contempt, sarcasm, admiration, or intimacy.

THE V/T SYSTEM AND THE JAPANESE HONORIFIC LANGUAGE SYSTEM

Interestingly, almost all the generalizations about V and T above, made by Brown and Gilman, apply to Japanese as well if we consider as V the polite *desu/-masu* style of speech and as T the non-polite or plain *da* style of speech. V, then, would correspond in the text to all P levels, while T corresponds to the N level. There are also some differences.

Similarities

Just as speakers of these European languages must make a choice between V and T when speaking to someone, the Japanese also must make a choice between the informal *da* style and the formal *desu/-masu* style, based on the relationship between the speaker and the addressee. The two dimensions involved in the use of the *da* style and the *desu/-masu* style, hierarchy and intimacy, directly correspond to power and solidarity in the V/T system.

One point, however, needs to be clarified. The use of the term "solidarity" in the sense of "degree of intimacy" may be a bit confusing with regard to the group-oriented Japanese. The Japanese group is solidary, but it is within that very group that the power semantic prevails. To avoid the confusion, Brown and Gilman's term "solidarity" will hereafter be replaced by the term "intimacy" in reference to the Japanese.

In the European system, the extensive use of V was considered a mark of elegance and was associated with the upper class in the past. In Japan, too, equals of the upper class exchanged mutual P, while people of the lower class exchanged mutual N. The ability to manipulate *keigo* with all its complexity was associated with a higher socio-economic background and better education, and continues to be so to this day. The degree of refinement in speech, as evidenced in the facility to use *keigo*, becomes an index of the speaker's upbringing, particularly in the case of women, who are expected to speak more politely than men. Social climbers, therefore, often try to pass as having come from a good family background by using overly polite speech.

The sudden code switching from the customary V to T, or T to V in European languages finds its equivalent in Japanese also. It is not uncommon in Japanese households for the wife to deviate from her norm and use an overly polite style (as if her husband were a lord) in response to his bossy behavior. A sudden switch to an extremely cruder or extremely more polite style is rather effective in expressing, often sarcastically, the speaker's change in mood.

Differences

Linguistically, there are qualitative and quantitative differences. In the V/T system of the European languages, one is forced to make a choice whether to use V or T as the second person pronoun with regard to the particular addressee, while in Japanese one has to make the choice in style—whether to use the informal *da* style or the formal *desu/-masu* style. Therefore, whereas sentences that do not contain a second person pronoun can be expressed neutrally in European languages, in Japanese, even these sentences must be expressed either in the informal *da* or the formal *desu/-masu* style. The result is that sentences that have nothing to do with the addressee "you," are subjected to this choice, such as between *Shizuka da* (It is quiet) and *Shizuka desu* or between *Ame ga futte iru* (It is raining) and *Ame ga futte imasu*. Once the choice of style is made with regard to a particular conversational partner, generally the style is adhered to consistently.

There is another important linguistic difference. The European V/T is an either/or choice, while, as we have seen, the *desu/-masu* style in Japanese has many gradations. European languages do not have lexical substitutes for neutral nouns and verb roots as Japanese does. Nor can one express respect in European languages while speaking in T, as one can in the nonpolite *da* style.

In today's Europe, the use of T, on the other hand, applies broadly to all fellow students, fellow workers, members of the same political group, etc., unlike in the very narrow category of "equal" in Japanese society. In Japan it is precisely within the highly organized groups that would connote solidarity in Europe, such as school sports clubs and political groups, where rank is strictly observed and the power semantic prevails.

One more difference from the European V/T system is that in Japanese, honorific words can be used in referring to a third person whom one holds in high esteem or whom one ought to show respect to, such as one's teacher or the Emperor. The application of respect terms to a third person does not exist in Europe because the V/T distinction can only be made with regard to the second person.

Despite these differences, the semantic similarity between the European V/T system and the Japanese system is impressive. In both systems, one must obligatorily select between V and T or N and P. In both systems, two factors are at work: power or status difference, and degree of intimacy, with the result that T or N implies condescension or intimacy, V or P reverence or formality.

REFERENCES

Brown, R., & Gilman, A. The pronouns of power and solidarity. In T. A. Sebeok (Ed.) *Style in Language*. Cambridge, Mass.: The M.I.T.Press, 1960, pp. 253-276.

Dunbar, E. N. How to say 'give' and 'receive' in Japanese: A preliminary study. *Working Papers in Linguistics*, University of Hawaii, 1973, 5, 11, pp. 1-139.

Goldstein, B. Z., & Tamura, K. *Japan and America: A Comparative Study in Language and Culture*. Rutland, Vt., & Tokyo: Charles E. Tuttle, 1975.

Mizutani, O., & Mizutani, N. *How to Be Polite in Japanese*. The Japan Times, 1987.

Monbusho. *Kore kara no Keigo* (Honorific Language Hereafter). In Bunkacho (Ed.) *Kotoba Shiriizu* (Language Series) No. 1, 1974, pp. 83-88.

Nakane, C. *Japanese Society*. Berkeley, CA: University of California Press, 1970.

Suzuki, T. *Words in Context*. A. Miura (Tr.) Tokyo: Kodansha International, 1984.

Tsujimura, T. *Keigo no shinsetsu na tsukaikata*. In Bunkacho (Ed.), *Kotoba Shiriizu 24*: *Zoku Keigo* (Language Series No. 24: Honorific Language, Continued). Okurasho Insatsukyoku, 1986.

INDEX

A

acquaintance, 40, 142. *See also* non-intimates

address term: definition, 74; for family members, 91–93, 98–99; general rules, 76–82; male/female differences at N-level, 49; in P-1, review, 132; for out-group person, chart, 107

Africans, 24

age: as determinant of status, 20, 38; of Japanese, estimating, 22–23

ageru. See donatory verbs

aka no tanin, 27

American English, politeness gradation in, 13–14; polite command, 138

Americans: category of equals, 19; ignoring *keigo*, 40, 138. *See also* Caucasians; foreigners; non-Japanese; non-native speakers; Westerners

anata: misuse of, 14, 76; Ministry of Education recommendation, 14; at N-level, 84–85, 137; non-use at P-level, 74–75, 76, 84, 132; overuse by foreigners, 74; at P-O by men, 88; use by *meue* to *meshita*, 40

anta, 84, 87

-are-/-rare-: as exalting form, 55–57, 60–62, 72, 135–136; as passive form, 56–57

Asians, 24

atashi, 87

B

bank, speaking to clerk at, 142

basic rule, 16, 27. *See also* in-group/out-group principle

benefactor, speaking to, 139–140

boku, 50, 87

boss: reference to, in-group & out-group, 29, 89–90; younger, 22
Brown, Roger, 151, 152–153
business card, 26

C

Caucasian, race 24; as visitor, 30. *See also* Americans; foreigners; non-Japanese;
  non-native speakers; Westerners
causative verb, 125–128
-chan, -chama, 82, 99
chiji, as tile, 79
children: group orientation of, 26–27; showing respect to elders, 19; speaking to,
  101–102, 103, 144
Chinese compounds, 36, 38, 134
-choo, 77, 78
choodai, 128–129
circumlocution, 33
classmates, as intimates, 40
client, speaking to, 29, 144
code switching, 154
commercial establishments, speaking to service people at, 142
compliments, 49
condescension, V or T of, 38, 39, 152
conferences, speaking at, 19
cohesion, in levels, 131
co-occurrence restriction, 131
cross-cultural communication, 33

D

da style: definition, 36; in relation to group & hierarchy, 38–39. *See also* N
daijin, as title, 79
degree of politeness. *See* levels
demonstratives, 71–72, 133
democratization, 18, 148
dentist, speaking to, 140
dependency, of Japanese, 20, 31
deru kui wa utareru, 27
desu/-masu style: definition, 36; in relation to group & hierarchy, 38–39. *See also* P
direct speech, 33
doctor, speaking to, 140

donatory verbs, 31–32, 108–131

-domo, 105

doohai, 21–22

double exaltation, 48

double use of donatory verbs, 120–122

drinking parties, speech at, 40

du, German, 138, 151

E

education institution, 29. *See also* university setting

elders in family, definition, 98

embedded sentence, 48, 120–121

emotional reaction, 14–16. *See also* status conscious Japanese

emperor, special vocabulary for, 149

equals, category of, 19, 25

equalization, of human relationship, 148

ethnicity, 24

euphemism, 33

European languages, 138, 151–155

exalting terms: donatory verbs, 110–111; nouns, 63–66; verbs, 52–57

F

F, 45

F+, 45

family: in-group/out-group distinction, 28; pre- and post-war differences, 146; within, P or N? 147. *See also* kinship terms

faux pas, 16, 74

favors: as determinant of status, 24; & obligation, 30–32

feeling of speaker: in choice of donatory verb, 118–119, 123–124; in code switching, 154

female speech: donatory verbs, 113; male/female differences, 49–51; at N-level, 47; noun with honorific prefix, 64, 66–67, 68, 73; speaking to lower status people, 145

first name (FN), 81, 82

first person pronoun. *See* "I"

FN, 81, 82

foreigners: apologizing ahead of time, 16; of Japanese ancestry, 24; non-use of *keigo* by, 14–16, 138; as out-group members, 30; permanently living in Japan, 17; pronunciation, 17; use of *sasete itadaku*, 125–128. *See also* Amer-

icans; Caucasians; non-Japanese; non-native speakers; Westerners
formality: definition, 36; at P-1 & P-2, 47; V of, 152
frankness, in relation to politeness, 16
friendship: junior-senior relationship in, 25; non-intimate, 143; termination of,
    14–15; use of N-level in, 40

G

-gata, 105
gift giving, & obligation, 30–32. See also *giri*
Gilman, Albert, 151, 152–153
giri, 30, 108
giving & receiving, verbs of. *See* donatory verbs
go-, honorific prefix, 63–68
Goldstein, Bernice Z., 109
government officer, speaking to, 142
gozaimasu, 41–42, 134–135. *See also* P-2
gradation of politeness. *See* levels
grammarians, 36, 48
guest, 19, 30

H

harmony, 27
heads of lower divisions, 78–79. See also *-choo*
hierarchy: & status, 18–25, 38; of in-group in relation to out-group, 29
hito, 46, 72
honorific language system, definition, 35
honorifics, definition, 35
hospital, 29, 78
host family: speaking to members of, 143; speaking to parents of, 140
humbling: basic rule, 27; donatory verbs, 111; mono, 72; verbs, 52–55, 58–62

I

"I": at different levels, 47; sentences without, 47; in speaking to children,
    101–102; in speaking to out-group persons, chart, 106; unnecessary use of,
    75–76; various first person pronouns, 87–88
identification, in use of donatory verbs, 116–121
identity, 25–27
ikkoo/go-ikkoo, 105
incomplete sentences, 33

indirect speech, 33

in-group interaction, observation of hierarchy, 52

in-group/out-group distinction, 27; relativity of, 89–90; postwar change in, 149. See also *uchi* and *yoso*

in-goup/out-group principle: as basic rule, 27; definition, 52; with non-intimate friends, 142; in use of donatory verbs, 109–115, 130

in-laws, speaking to, 92–93, 100

insulting addressee, by use of: *anata*, 15, 74, 76; direct speech, 33; N-level speech, 40; wrong donatory verb, 118

intimacy, T of, 152

intimate equals, 40, 143–144

itadakeru, potential of *itadaku*, 127–128

itadaku. See donatory verbs

J

Japanese blood, 24

jimuin, 21

juunishi, 21

K

kanojo, 88–89

kare, 88–89

kata, 47, 72

keigo words: classification of, 36; definition, 35; implications of non-use, 138

keigo no midare, 148

keigo system, 35–36, 137–139

kenjoo-go, 36, 52. *See also* humbling

kimi: devaluation of, 75; non-use within family, 101; use of, 44, 84, 85, 136

kinship terms, 91–93; fictive use of, 104

kisama, 75

koohai, 21, 142. See also *sempai*

kone, 31

ko-, so-, a-, do- words, 70–72

kudasai, 139

kudasaru. See donatory verbs

-kun, 81–82, 101

kureru. See donatory verbs

L

last name (LN) 80, 81, 82, 133; plus -*san*, 80, 132

lawyer, speaking to, 140

levels, of politeness: 37–38, 41–44; in American English, 13–14; recommendation of Ministry of Education re, 149; sample sentences, 42, 45–49; use of, 131–148

M

M, male speech (at N-level), 44

macho, way of speaking, 50

mairu, 47, 97

male/female speech: differences, 49–51, 64, 145; level of politeness, 47; sample sentences, 42, 45–47

mama, 95

meshita: "giving to, 112; speaking to, 144–145; at work settings, 20. See also *meue*

meue: category of, 140–142; complimenting, 49; speaking to, 139–141; at work settings, 21; use of *anata* by, 40

mina-san/-sama, 106–107

Ministry of Education, 14, 148

morau. See donatory verbs

N

N: definition, 36; use of, general, 39–40, 41–47; with respect verb by women, 44; review, 136, 146–150. See also *da* style

Nakane, Chie, 19

negative questions, 43, 128

neutral sentences, 44, 47, 154

non-intimates: category of, 142; friends, 141-142; as out-group members, 25

non-Japanese, fluent in Japanese, 15–16. *See also* Americans; Caucasians; foreigners; non-native speakers; Westerners

non-native speakers: & indirect communication, 33; wrong choice of donatory verb 115. *See also* Americans; Caucasians; foreigners; non-Japanese; Westerners

nonverbal communication, 32-35

O

o-: honorific prefix, 63, 64–66; at N-level by women, 51, 136; essential at P-1, 132

o-age suru. See donatory verbs

obligations. See *giri*

*o-*____ *desu*, exalting verb, 57

ofukuro, 97

OL, 21

omae: devaluation of, 75; use of, 85, 101

on, and *giri*, 108

on-, honorific prefix, 63, 65, 66

*o-*___ ni naru, exalting verb, 55, 56

ore, 87

*o-*___ *suru*, humbling verb, 58–60, 73

otaku, 85–86

oyaji, 97

P

P: definition, 36; as level, 41–49; use of, 40, 153. *See also desu/-masu-* style

P-O: definition 45; use of, 142–143, 144. *See also* P

P-1: definition, 45; use of, 139–142, 142–143; components of, 131–133. *See also* P

P-2: definition, 45; characteristics of, 133–136. See also P

papa, 99

particles: post-position, articulation of, 134; omission at N level, 136; at end of
    sentence, 50–51

passive, 125

perception, 18

plurality, 104–106

policeman, speaking to, 143

post office, speaking to clerk of, 142

power semantic, 151

politeness: definition, 37–38; gradation of, see levels

postwar: democratization 18, 148; in-group/out-group distinction, 29, 149; use of
    kare, *kanojo*, 88–89. *See also* prewar

prefix, honorific, 63–70, 132

prewar: guidance in *keigo*, 146; observation of hierarchy, 18, 149; teacher, 39.
    See also postwar

pronoun: first person (*see* "I"); second person (*see* "You"); third person, 88–89;
    possessive, 87

pupils, speaking to, 144

R

race, as determinant of status, 24

ALL ABOUT KATAKANA
Anne Matsumoto Stewart
This book helps students read and write *katakana* in the shortest and most rational way possible.
ISBN 4-7700-1696-4; paperback; 144 pages

ALL ABOUT PARTICLES
Naoko Chino
Helps students discover new particles and remember the old ones, while learning proper usage.
ISBN 4-7700-1501-1; paperback; 128 pages

BEYOND POLITE JAPANESE
Akihiko Yonekawa
A concise, pocket-sized reference full of expressions that all Japanese, but few foreigners, know and use every day.
ISBN 4-7700-1539-9; paperback; 176 pages

"BODY" LANGUAGE
Jeffrey G. Garrison
Helps students learn common idioms that refer to the body. Students will learn to stop paraphrasing and get straight to the point.
ISBN 4-7700-1502-X; paperback; 128 pages

FLIP, SLITHER, & BANG
Hiroko Fukuda/Translated and edited by Tom Gally
Introduces the most common examples of onomatopoeia through sample sentences and actual situations.
ISBN 4-7700-1684-0; paperback; 128 pages

GONE FISHIN'
Jay Rubin
Explains, clarifies, and illuminates the perennial trouble spots of the Japanese language in a humorous manner.
ISBN 4-7700-1656-5; paperback; 128 pages

INSTANT VOCABULARY Through Prefixes and Suffixes
Timothy J. Vance
With this book, students can upgrade their level of speech and learn to create new words from existing vocabulary.
ISBN 4-7700-1500-3; paperback; 128 pages

HOW TO SOUND INTELLIGENT
Charles M. De Wolf
Lists, defines, and gives examples for the vocabulary necessary to engage in intelligent conversations in various fields.
ISBN 4-7700-1747-2; paperback; 128 pages